GOD'S WORLD

Trevor Huddleston was born in Bedford in 1913, and was educated at Lancing and Christ Church, Oxford. The social problems of England in the early 1930s quickly awoke an interest in missionary work, and he went to Ceylon and India before studying at Wells Theological College.

He was ordained in 1937, and in 1943 went to South Africa as Priest-in-Charge of the Community of the Resurrection's Mission in Sophiatown. He stayed in South Africa until 1956, and has been a champion of the black people there ever since.

In 1958 Trevor Huddleston became Prior of the London House of the Community of the Resurrection; in 1960 Bishop of Masasi, South Africa, and in 1968 Bishop of Stepney, in London. He then became Bishop of Mauritius and Archbishop of the Province of the Indian Ocean in 1978. He returned to England in 1983, where he continues to be active in the struggle against apartheid.

His most famous book, *Naught for Your Comfort*, one of the earliest writings to alert people in the West to the plight of non-whites in South Africa, was first published in 1956.

D1381979

Books by the same author available
as Fount Paperbacks

I BELIEVE
NAUGHT FOR YOUR COMFORT

GOD'S WORLD

Trevor Huddleston C.R.

Collins
FOUNT PAPERBACKS

First published in Great Britain by
Fount Paperbacks, London in 1988

Copyright © Trevor Huddleston 1988

Printed and bound in Great Britain by
William Collins Sons & Co Ltd, Glasgow

The material in this book was originally given in the form
of addresses to two groups of university people in the 1960s.
The material in chapters 1-8 was delivered at the University
College of Makerere, Uganda, in 1964; that in chapters 9-10
formed part of the basis of a Mission to Oxford University in the
Hilary Term of 1963.
It was all subsequently published in *God's World* (Fontana, 1966)
and in *The True and Living God* (Fontana, 1964) respectively.

INTRODUCTION

This book originated a quarter of a century ago in an invitation from Oxford to conduct a week's mission to the University. It was a challenge I could not refuse, but it was a daunting challenge all the same. I was, at the time, Bishop of Masasi in Tanzania, and I had no direct contact with Oxford and no real knowledge of the state of religion in the University. I had to rely on the information provided by College Chaplains and undergraduates. But I had the great advantage of living in a newly independent African country already discovering its own identity as a nation: a nation led by Julius Nyerere; a nation which, being part of God's World, had much to contribute to a better understanding of God's World. So I wrote the addresses which form part of this book.

Soon afterwards another University, this time Makerere in Uganda, called upon me to lead a mission there. It would need to be a totally different kind of mission to a widely different audience of students who would in time provide leadership to the whole of East Africa. (No hint then of the coming of Idi Amin and his assault on all academic and civilized values.) So it would have to look to the future – the immediate future. Having delivered those addresses I can truthfully say that I never read them again until now. I assumed they would be irrelevant and outdated.

So I was both surprised and deeply grateful to the publishers to be told otherwise and to discover that, after all, the truths I was trying to communicate to the students of that generation still have meaning for today.

I can only say that in the subsequent years my conviction has deepened concerning a truth I then only dimly grasped and even more dimly responded to. The titles "God's World" and "The True and Living God" which I chose for my themes at Oxford and Makerere are really only *one* theme. And this theme has become more relevant now than it was in the early sixties.

It is, quite simply, that because this *is* God's World and not ours, we need to get back to the primal vision expressed in the word "Creation". For the doctrine of Creation must have priority over all other doctrines if Christianity is to express the purpose of the True and Living God for His world. The first verses of the first chapter of the first book of the Bible spell it out: "In the beginning God *created*. . . ."

If this small book can do anything to spread this Word I shall be more than content.

London   Trevor Huddleston +
March 1988

CONTENTS

Preface

It will be clear to anyone reading these addresses that I have drawn very extensively on three books: *The Christian Faith* by F.W. Dillistone (Hodder & Stoughton) (especially for the ideas in chapter 3); *Saving Belief* by Austin Farrer (Hodder & Stoughton) (especially for chapters 4 and 5); and *The Church and the Reality of Christ* by John Knox (Collins).

Because I can make no claim to originality of thought, I am in no way ashamed of having used the ideas and the wisdom of such teachers as these. I am very grateful to them for their inspiration, and I ask their forgiveness if I have in any way misinterpreted their thoughts.

It is sometimes said that communication is the biggest problem confronting the Christian evangelist in post-Christian Europe. I believe it to be no less a problem in the Africa which is now finding its own place in the world. And I do not for one moment think that, in these addresses, I have solved such a problem. All I can say is that I have made an attempt.

TREVOR HUDDLESTON C.R.
Bishop of Masasi
1965

1

God and Our World

I would like to discuss a question: a question common to man as man. Put simply and briefly it is this: "What does it all *mean*?" It is this question of meaning which drives the human race forward. It is the spur in every field of human activity. It is the question which moves the scientist and the artist, the historian and the philosopher, the worker and the ruler. "What does it mean?"

As somebody has written penetratingly:

> The human institution which has symbol-
> ized this search for meaning, coherence,
> integration, wisdom, has been the univer-
> sity. Its very name relates it to that which
> is universal. Its activities, carried on in
> many different departments, ideally focus
> attention upon one question: Is there any
> single meaning to this whole vast mass
> of accumulated knowledge? Or, to put it
> another way. When the world of nature
> and the long record of history have yielded
> up their secrets and these have been care-
> fully stored and tabulated, do they include
> anything distinctive which can constitute

a principle of integration and therefore an indication of meaning?[1]

"What does it all mean?" That is the question which has created the universities of the world, and it is also the question which, *in* this world, can never be finally answered. Life is too great and too wonderful to be held within the forms and categories which the human mind and intellect can fashion. But you are here nevertheless because you want to know the meaning of it all. And this University College, of which you are a part, exists for the very purpose of helping you in your quest, and uses all its resources to this end. To use a sixteenth-century metaphor, "The universities are the *eyes* of the land."[2] If the eyes of a society are put out or even blinkered, that society begins to stumble and ultimately falls—"When there is no vision, the people perish."

And I am here as a Christian to speak about the *meaning* of things. Not because I am so foolish as to think that I know all the answers. Not because I think I have some special experience of life which is richer or wider or fuller than that of others. Least of all because I think that Western civilization is in itself superior to any other known form of civilization. No. I come to speak about the meaning of things—of our world, of man, of freedom, of sin and evil, of death

[1] F.W. Dillistone, *The Christian Faith* (Hodder & Stoughton, 1964), p.38.
[2] Dillistone, p.131.

and life and continuing fellowship—because the Christian faith which I profess is also a catholic faith; that is to say, a faith concerned with universals. Or, to put it more simply and in a more contemporary phrase, because the Christian faith claims to be *relevant* to every single facet of human existence; because the Christian must say (at the point of being false to his profession if he doesn't) that there is nothing in the whole wide world, nothing in the whole universe, which lies outside the range of God's care and of God's concern. "The Lord's is the earth and its fullness, the world and all its peoples. It is he who set it on the seas; on the waters he made it firm. . . ." In saying so much the Christian is saying no more than the Jew, no more than the follower of the Prophet is able to say. It is the proclamation that God is the Creator and Ruler of the universe; that it is in relation to him alone that it has meaning and purpose. That it is because there is one God, and he the Creator, the Alpha and the Omega, that any meaning exists at all. It is to say that because God the Omnipotent holds the universe in the hollow of his hand, the forces which move that universe are under control—*his* control; are not just blind chance, purposeless flux, chaos and darkness beneath an appearance of order. And this is to say a great deal. For it is the affirmation that there is *meaning* in the universe. It is the assurance that man's unceasing quest for meaning is worth while; is, quite literally, *infinitely* worth while. But it is *not* to say that the human intellect, nor even the combination of all human intellectual effort, can achieve the final answer. If it could it would be the divine, omniscient intellect itself. If it could, humanity would be God.

The Christian faith proclaims unequivocally that the universe, and this world as part of the universe, has meaning because it is God's universe, God's world. But it makes a far greater and more stupendous claim than this. The heart of the Christian faith is what we Christians call the Gospel—the proclamation of good news. And the good news is nothing less than this: that God, the One, the Creator and Sustainer of the universe, has entered the world he made. The Bible opens: "In the beginning God. . . ." For the Christian it continues: and GOD became MAN. "In the beginning was the Word . . ." and the Word was with God and the Word was God, "all things were made by him, and without him was not anything made that was made." "I believe in One God, maker of heaven and earth . . ." AND THE WORD WAS MADE FLESH AND DWELT AMONG US. This is the event which, so Christians claim, opens up a whole new dimension of *meaning* to mankind. For if the Creator of the world has himself entered the world, not only, so to speak, touching it but identifying himself with it as man, he brings—or *reveals*—the meaning of existence with him. This is the claim which the Christian faith makes. Nothing less, nothing other; that in the person of Jesus Christ God shows the meaning of human life. Or, to put it more concretely, in the Person of

Jesus Christ is all that mankind *can* know about God's meaning for itself. He does not merely point a way of living and behaving which is good; he *is* the Way. He does not merely express a truth about human existence; he *is* the Truth. He does not merely tell mankind the most satisfactory goals to aim at in life; he *is* the Life.

It is in this sense that the Christian faith claims to be relevant to our world. Because a university is concerned above all else with discovering the meaning of things, it is not, after all, impertinent for a Christian to play his part. And even if it were, he would still be constrained to do so at his Master's command. But there are two warnings I wish to give before I begin. First, and most obviously, the message I have to proclaim is infinitely greater than the words I shall be able to use for its proclamation. I may utterly fail to convey the truth because of my own limitations. Secondly, I am bound to be influenced in the way I proclaim the message by my own experience of the Christian faith—in its English as well as its African context—as a Minister of God in the Anglican Church.

*

We are to think about God and our world. My introduction has been long precisely because one cannot begin to think about this topic unless we have first cleared the ground and shown why Christianity claims to have anything to say on the subject, and on what foundation that claim may rest. Christianity, in claiming to be the catholic faith, claims to have relevance to every part and problem of human existence. That is a stupendous claim for any faith to make. Christianity makes it on the ground of one, historical *event*. And it all began in a stable!

Consider for a moment the course of things which led to that event—the path in historical terms which led to the stable: "There went out a decree from Caesar Augustus that all the world should be enrolled ... it was in the days when Cyrenius was Governor of Syria. . . ."

From Rome to that far-off colony, and to every other colony, the order came. The state is not interested in persons as persons. It was not concerned with individuals or families, and because in that particular colony, at that particular moment, it was most convenient administratively to use the tribal unit, "everyone went to his own town"—to the place of his fathers. Joseph and Mary, we are told, went to Bethlehem, being of David's tribe. They were part of the crowd. So much a part of the crowd that when they came to find a lodging there was no room for them anywhere. And so they took refuge in a stable. That was the pattern. That, so far as historical records go, was the *whole* pattern. A decree from the head of state; machinery set in motion by the local governor and his regional commissioners; a form to fill in; a new number to be added to the thousands on the census file: "Three from Nazareth. Tribe: David's. Trade: Carpenter." And somewhere, back in Rome, it was pigeon-holed for future reference and eventually discarded because it was out of date.

And yet it was the stable that mattered and that changed the course of history, not the act of Caesar. It was the stable that threw its light back and gave meaning to the act of the Emperor. It was the stable, you might say, which alone made the act even memorable. Without the stable and the event which happened there that bit of history would have no significance whatever. It would not have existed. On any showing, on any interpretation of that moment in history—not the Christian interpretation only—the stable was a more important place than the palace of Caesar Augustus.

At Masasi the older building, and the stronger, is not the Cathedral but the Chapter house. It used to be a stable. And because of the wildness of the country round about, its windows are narrow, to prevent leopards marauding. Its walls are strong rock. It has endured. "There was no room for Mary and Joseph at the inn"—but they found shelter and protection in a stable. Forget the picture on the Christmas card or the words of the carol for a moment, and think rather of a strong protective wall of rock. Think of a place built to keep out the marauder and to keep warm inside the cattle and the sheep. This was the stable at Bethlehem—this is the stable everywhere; a refuge for the weak, the helpless, the unprotected. And what could be more defenceless, more totally dependent, than a new-born baby? "There was no room. . . ." "He came unto his own, and his own received him not"—but the stable was there, the place of refuge and of compassion. The world takes a long time to learn the meaning of compassion, of caring, of succouring the weak. But because of the stable, and I would even dare to say *only* because of the stable, and the event, the birth, the baby within it, the idea of compassion has found its embodiment in history. What, after all, is a hospital or a school for the blind or a refugee camp but a stable? And why does it exist if sickness or blindness or helplessness are just accidents in a meaningless game called life?

That stable was shelter also for a *family*: "Mary and Joseph and the babe lying in a manger." A family which, at the time, was so much part of the crowd that the inn-keeper saw in it nothing but trouble to himself. A pregnant woman and her man—that was all. No room in the inn. But the family in the stable is the family on which a whole civilization has been built. That stable is the place where motherhood is seen as something grounded in purity as well as love; where fatherhood is recognized as needing charity and obedience, as well as authority. Society—that is the whole social order—has been penetrated by the light shining out. It is the stable that has given meaning to society; not the reverse.

And then the shepherds! The first to recognize the meaning of the stable; the first to know what had really happened there. Sometimes, in hymns and in Bible study, we are tempted to think of the shepherds as representing the simple and the unlearned. But the qualities of a shepherd are not just simplicity and ignorance.

We have quite a number of young shepherds in Masasi, mostly children out of school too early, earning a few shillings by spending the day with a neighbour's herd of sheep or goats. Usually they are more ragged and more dirty than their contemporaries in the classroom. Often they are not in church on Sundays but out on the hills. It is a whole-time job, done cheerfully and with little reward. But what it demands is watchfulness—watchfulness and caring.

So the shepherds of Bethlehem, when they came to the stable, knew the meaning of what had happened there before the wise men or anyone else. The stable was familiar ground to them; it was, you might say, their home and their workshop, their school and their playground. And now it became their place of worship also.

I have chosen the stable as my symbol because it covers the meaning of that event which Christians call the Incarnation; the en-fleshment; the coming-down-to-earth of the one, almighty and all-holy God. This event is the foundation of the whole Christian faith. The baby in the manger is "Very God of very God" and "true man". Without this assertion as to the meaning of Jesus there is no meaning whatsoever in the Christian Gospel. Unless the stable shelters the "Word made flesh" it has no significance whatsoever—nor has the story which the gospels tell; nor has the faith which the Christian Church has professed for two thousand years and by which it still lives. Indeed, unless the Christian Church is part of that very event in the stable, the Christian Church has no meaning either.

But if that baby is the Person the Church believes him to be, then the stable is the place where we can discover *meaning*: the meaning of history; the meaning of man; the meaning of society; the meaning of life.

The stable, we believe, is the centre of all history, "in the sense that the horizontal movement of human affairs [all that we understand by the historical process] was uniquely touched at that point by a vertical inflow from above".[3] "Great little one whose lowly *birth* lifts earth to heaven, stoops heaven to earth." It is not because the event or even the Person made any impact on contemporary documents that it is a unique moment in history. The incarnation of God "left scarcely a mark on secular records . . . yet, however far from the focus of public history Jesus moved, the human existence of Jesus was a focus drawing the world into itself".[4] By taking flesh of Mary, by entering fully and completely into human existence at its weakest and its most dependent, God gives to man a dignity, and therefore a meaning, which is unique. The stable shelters a new-born baby in all his helplessness. But if that frail flesh

[3] A. Farrer, *Saving Belief*, (Hodder & Stoughton, 1964), p.69.
[4] *idem*.

is the flesh of God, if manhood is truly "taken into God" by this act, then man the person, man the individual, man as man matters *infinitely*. Christianity alone gives to man this immeasurable dignity. It is the only true humanism.

The stable also shelters a family—the Holy Family we call it. And in consequence of this, Christianity asserts that a social order, a society which ignores or debases the true dignity of the family, is in fact destroying society itself. The stable shelters a family; a very ordinary artisan family of the large tribe of David. But if that family is in fact the chosen way of God's entering human society, the family itself and the ties which bind it together have a meaning and a purpose which are also infinite.

But it was the shepherds who came first to the stable. And they came, we are told, straight from work, "keeping watch over their flocks by night". They were doing the job they knew—perhaps the only job they knew; living the life they had chosen—perhaps the life that had been chosen for them. They were "keeping watch", ready, alert, prepared—but not for anything except the lion or the wolf—when "the glory of the Lord shone all about them".

Why was it only the shepherds who found their way into that stable, I wonder? Why they who saw GLORY? Can it have been because, although the door was low, they were not afraid to bend and kneel?

2

Why the Church?

In my first address we were trying to think about the foundation on which the Christian claim to uniqueness and to universality rests. And we found it to lie in the fact that God, all-holy, almighty, Creator and Sustainer of the universe, has entered into his creation and has identified himself with man. It is the stable, and the event which happened there, that gives meaning to history, to man, to society and to life itself.

It is somehow in relation to this Person, to God made flesh, that this fantastic claim is made. Now we must move on a stage further and try to discover honestly and without evasion *how* this event is relevant to us.

In the first place it happened so very long ago. Although two thousand years is not long in comparison with the time-span of the whole human race, it is immensely long in terms of the life-span of an individual. And we are individuals. Just because it was an historical event, not a legend or a myth or a fairy story, it is inescapably linked with its own period and with Caesar Augustus and the Roman hegemony; with a particular race, the Jewish people, whose own history is sharply different at every point from ours; with a way of life shaped and formed by economic and social patterns totally different from those which influence our own life in Africa or Europe in the twentieth century. *Distance*, whether in time or space, may lend enchantment, may make a story appeal to our emotions or our intellect, but it also separates us utterly from the event itself. That Jesus of Nazareth *was* an historical figure we cannot doubt. Certainly no other has been subject to the attention and research of scholars in every field over so many centuries. But is it possible for him and in that distant context to mean anything, to be relevant in any degree, to a generation like ours and to the generations which will follow ours?

Secondly, if the Christian claim be true, does not its very uniqueness make it more difficult? Not just more difficult for our intelligence, but more difficult for our moral sense, to accept? Jesus of Nazareth is, by all measurements and standards, so *different* from the rest of mankind; so different in his nature and in his claims; he is, we are told, both God and man—and therefore he must surely stand outside human experience rather than within it. How can he reach me, let alone help me—I who stand so firmly within my own human nature, who know so well my own weakness and blindness and limitation?

And, finally, just because the truth about Jesus of Nazareth has reached me through written records of such antiquity, and because those records are admittedly only a fragment of what might have been written about him, how can I be sure that this unique event has reached me as it really was? How can I be sure that I see this figure as the shepherds saw him in the stable, or as his followers saw him in the villages and by the lake shore—when the only records of their experience were written so long after the event and when so much of the record was never written at all? Jesus was able to ask his disciples "What think ye of Christ?" and they could not evade the question with him standing there in front of them, flesh and blood. But what are we to say? What is the link between the Jesus of history and the modern world? What is it that joins that immensely distant and different moment in time with this moment? What is the reality, the actual present reality for Africa today, of that stupendous event, and where is it to be found?

It seems to me that there is only one possible answer to these questions, and one which I believe with all my heart: it is the Christian Church. *No other link.* And it seems to me, further, quite useless to consider the other great questions which confront us until we have honestly faced this one. For, to the Christian, there can be no answer outside the context of the Church to which he belongs. And to the non-Christian any answers which ignore the fact of the Church are dishonest answers. And so we ask *Why the Church*?

One of the problems still confronting Christianity in Africa today is that it is true, as Bishop Lesslie Newbigin once put it, that "The

Churches are to outward seeing very much like Western cultural colonies precariously situated on the edge of the old societies ... heavily dependent both spiritually and financially, on continuing support from the West... They show little power of spontaneous growth and depend rather upon a continual flow of resources from outside to keep them where they are. Though eyes of faith may see them as the first fruits of the people of Asia and Africa, eyes not so lighted will be inclined to write them off as the ineffectual remnants of the era of Western dominance. . . . "[1]

"The ineffectual remnants of the era of Western dominance." The Christian Church in Africa, however we define it and wherever we set its outer boundaries, is seen in this view as an *alien* institution. It is seen, further, as being linked to a past situation, described as "colonialism" or "exploitation". Most specifically it is seen as linked with a culture, a way of life and of looking at life, which is *not* African. Its buildings, its institutional forms, its literature, its music, all proclaim the same truth about it. It is alien. Therefore it cannot but be hostile to the great movement of nationalism or Africanism which is shaking the whole continent to its foundations, and in which the whole future of the race really lies.

But not only is the Christian Church alien. It has embodied its ideas in an *institutional* form. It wouldn't be so bad, perhaps, if its alienation

[1] *The Relevance of Trinitarian Doctrine for Today's Mission*, (Edinburgh House Press), p.30.

from the African way of life were restricted to the realm of ideas. But, wherever the Church has penetrated African society it has set up a society of its own; a visible society, a distinct society with its own outward symbols, its own particular forms, its own laws governing behaviour and manners and human relationships. And, because it is an institution with fixed and rigid boundaries, it has an *exclusiveness* about it which perpetuates its alienation from the rest—from those outside the walls. The educational effort of the Christian Church in Africa has been stupendous; but it has also been directed at the presentation of the institution itself, so that even knowledge appears to be confined within certain fixed categories.

And this Western and alien culture which the Christian Church has brought to Africa is itself *divisive*, for it reflects only too clearly the cultural divisions of Western Europe. Isn't it almost nonsense to talk of "the Christian Church" when, in fact, the claim to be the Church is disputed among so many? When, as Africa shows so plainly, the ancient and irrelevant historic feuds of European Christians can be perpetuated and even revived in a totally new and innocent context?

Finally, is not the very existence of the Christian Church as an institution a denial of all that Christ himself and his coming into the world should mean? "God is a Spirit, and they that worship him must worship him in spirit and in truth." "In spirit . . ."; not in these material forms; not by using a vast organization; temples made of stone; and within the temples a hierarchy of ministers, a system and a protocol; forms of worship which involve, for instance, the use of bread and wine. Is not all this a denial of the spiritual nature of religion itself which Jesus came to proclaim? Is not the Church, the historic, institutional, material Church which claims to represent him, in fact a total contradiction of the Christian faith itself? And, if it is, what possible place exists for it in Africa today?

I have tried to state as forcefully as I can, and as clearly as I can understand them, some basic objections to the Christian Church in its African context. It is alien; it is institutional; it is divisive; it is materialistic. And yet—indispensable. How, then, can it be at the same time the indispensable and appointed link with Christ himself? Where, in the Church as we know it and recognize it, is the reality of Christ—the Christ of the stable—to be found? At the risk of over-emphasis, let me stress the point of the question. We are not asking at this moment, what is *wrong* with the Church. We are asking why is the Church *necessary* to the message or Gospel of Christ.

And there is only one way of meeting and answering that question; it is by looking again at the Person of Jesus of Nazareth.

1. *He was in the world and the world was made by him and the world knew him not . . . he came unto his own and his own received*

him not. These are the words of John, known as
the beloved disciple. And as he looks back over
the years, and his mind's eye rests on Jesus; on
the stable; on the synagogue at Capernaum; on
Jerusalem; on the palace of Pilate and the hill
of Golgotha, this is his summary of the impact of
Jesus, of the place of Jesus: "the world knew him
not ... his own received him not" The story of
Christ is, at its deepest level, the story of rejection. "There was no room for them at the inn";
but the inn was in fact the world, the country, the
town, the village to which he had come. "Foxes
have holes and the birds of the air have nests, but
the Son of Man hath no where to lay his head." So
it was in the synagogue at Capernaum, when he
began to preach and they cast him out because of
what he claimed to be. So it was when he showed
his power in healing, in giving sight to the blind,
in restoring the paralytic: "they besought him to
depart out of their coast". So it was with those
who were closest to him in blood and in friendship: "his brethren believed not on him". This
pattern of *rejection* runs through every part of
the Christian Gospel and embraces all the figures
in it until at last, alone on that lonely cross, he
himself cries out, "My God, my God, why hast thou
forsaken me?"

"The Church is alien", we say. And we mean,
of course, that the *missionary* Church has often
failed to adapt itself and integrate itself into the
country to which it has come. It has. There
is ground for the deepest penitence over such

failure; for penitence, and for renewal. But, fundamentally, the Church is always alien; always a reproach and a stumbling-block to the world in which it is set; because it is the Church; the Body of Christ; the hands and feet and lips of Christ, who was "despised and rejected of men", who "came unto his own and his own received him not".

2. And yet this same Jesus, who was and knew himself to be rejected by his own and by the world into which he had come, was able to choose who should be with him as and how he willed. "He chose twelve . . . ": fishermen like Simon and Andrew, Levi the tax-collector, James and John and Philip and the rest. And all through the Gospel it is apparent that there is a company separated off from the rest; given to share in the secrets of his heart. Whether this company is seen as restricted to the twelve; whether it embraces a larger number of disciples; whether, as happened from time to time, it becomes even more restricted (Peter and James and John), it is unmistakably there; the story makes no sense without it. And those who belong to it are told they are "the salt of the earth . . . the city set on a hill . . . the inheritors of the twelve thrones". "In the world," they are told, "you will have tribulations. But be of good cheer, I have overcome the world." Be of good cheer . . . the gates of hell shall not prevail against you. The Church is too institutionalized, we say, and we mean, certainly, that the *missionary* Church has

often failed by emphasizing the outward structure, the institutional forms, the rigid boundaries at the expense of Love. No doubt it has. No doubt there is room for deep penitence here also at our failure in sensitiveness and perception; our blindness in not recognizing the difference between the institution and what it contains or expresses.

But, by its very nature the Church must reflect the mind of its Master; of him who, whilst saying so explicitly, "Come unto me *all* ye who labour and are heavy laden . . .", whilst consorting with publicans and sinners, with Roman soldiers and Samaritans, with the outcasts of society, could yet choose, separate, mark out from the world those who were to be his representatives. The Church is institutional at its deepest level because the Lord made it so; because, in fact, in the world we know there is no other way of providing permanence and continuity and stability.

3. But the consequence of this "choosing", this "election"—if you want a more controversial theological term—is also inescapably division. "I am not come to bring peace," he said, "but a sword." And he warned those who would follow him that they would not only be separated from the *things* they loved ("Go and sell all you have and give to the poor") but from the people—from parents and brethren and friends. And that, without "hating" them, they could not be his disciples

It is true that the divisions *within* the Christian Church are both its gravest sin and failure and its greatest hindrance. It is divisive—where it should be unitive; a scandal where it should be a glory. And because of this divisiveness, we are told, the world cannot believe.

But if the Church is true to its Master, again it will compel a choice; it will be the enemy of all compromise; it will divide the false from the true, the dream from the reality, the darkness from the light.

4. Yet the one division which Christ never made, and which his Church can never make and still remain true to him, is the division between "spiritual" and "material". For this would be to deny the very fact on which the whole Gospel is based: the fact that God entered into his world by taking flesh, by becoming man and by using, in that perfect humanity, all the stuff of creation; all that we mean by "the material world". "Christianity is the most materialistic of all the great religions", as William Temple once said. And it is so because, in becoming man, God takes again the material world he has created—every part of it—and gives it a new meaning, a new reality.

It should not be surprising to us in Africa that the medium which he chooses for initiation into his Church is water. Nothing in Africa (nothing, for that matter, in his own land) so clearly enforces the meaning of life itself. Indeed it *is* life itself, both for the individual and for the community.

Some time ago a small group of boys appeared on my *baraza* at Masasi. They had come a long way and they were very hot and thirsty, and they asked for a drink of water. As each one received it he went down on his knee to drink. And when I asked them why, they said it was "for thanksgiving"—not to me, but simply for the gift itself; to the Giver. When Jesus came to the river to be baptized by John we are told that John wanted to refuse: "I had need to be baptized by you . . . " But Jesus himself said, "Suffer it to be so now, for thus it becometh us to fulfil all righteousness." "*To fulfil . . .* "

"The Law and the Prophets were until John . . ." but here is he who fulfils both Law and prophecy in his own person. Here is he who can say "I *am* the life". But he goes down into the water, and is baptized. And later, we are told, "being wearied with his journey, he sat by the well" and asked a Samaritan woman to draw water for him to drink. And later still he cried, "I thirst".

If the stable is the symbol of God's entering into history, water is the symbol of man's new life in Christ. And it is also the way, the means by which God *gives* man life; for it is the way into his Church.

In spite of the division which has obscured the meaning of this new life and a meaning which includes within itself the fact of its corporateness, baptism remains the common way of Christian initiation. Already, in ecumenical discussion and in the debates of the Vatican Council, it is recognized that here at least Christians share a divine gift, uniquely their own, creating a unity which no human folly or sinfulness can destroy.

But perhaps especially in Africa, where water and life are so interdependent, the meaning of baptism is easier to grasp. Because the need for water conditions the siting of a village, or its destruction; because the river or the spring or the well is in a true sense the very heart of society; because health and strength depend utterly on what water alone can bring, it is not difficult to see why it is also a condition of life in the family of God.

And because the obedience of the Son of God entailed, first, his going down into the river with John before he calls men to follow him, it is not hard to accept this same obedience for ourselves.

If we are wearied with our own journey, as we so often shall be, we have the same promise of living water to sustain us.

In the end, even if in our life as Christians there is the agony of failure and loss and disappointment, coming to the water brooks only to find them dry sand, we know that he has been there before us. He has shared our thirst. Why baptism? Why the Church? Because "by baptism we were buried with him and lay dead, in order that, as Christ was raised from the dead in the splendour of the Father, so also we might set our feet upon the new path of life."[2]

[2] Romans 6:4 (NEB).

3

What is Freedom?

There is little doubt that when the history of the
twentieth century comes to be written, the idea,
the obsession, one might almost say, which will
be seen to be at the heart of things, is the idea of
Freedom. Already it is possible, in European history, to see how in the nineteenth century men
had become engrossed with a different idea—the
idea of Progress. Almost everything was judged by
the one standard—did it make for progress or the
opposite? Almost everything, equally, that was
discovered or done or planned was regarded as
something contributing to progress. And Progress
itself—with a capital P—was seen as the ultimate
solution for all the ills of society and of the individual. "Only make progress—in education, in
art, in technical skill and the scientific discovery
of things—and all will be for the best in the best
of all possible worlds." It is easy to see, now, how
men confused the evolutionary idea with the idea
of progress. It seemed natural to think that any
advance in the control of the universe and its
properties would bring happiness. It seemed right
to believe that if man applied his reason effectively and diligently enough to the world around

him it must become a better, as well as a better-organized, world.

This illusion was shattered for us in the West by the First World War. A belief in automatic human progress has never been recovered since that catastrophic holocaust. The idea of progress in itself and by itself, without question; the end or the means, is seen as an illusion. What we of the twentieth century have to guard against is the danger of our idea of freedom, our near-obsession with freedom, going the same way.

In a sense it is because freedom is such a glorious word, with such a ring to it, that it can be so easily misused and debased. So it is worth while trying to discover whether Christianity, whether the Christian Church, has anything to say about it. And if so, whether what it has to say makes sense to us. It is important because, whilst other continents can *talk* about freedom, we in Africa are involved in it directly, existentially, every moment. And already we know, if we think at all, what a complex, multi-coloured, evasive idea it is. We know that to achieve the first stage—*Uhuru*, in the sense of freedom from colonialism—is in fact the simplest part of the process (not the easiest, necessarily; but the simplest to describe, the simplest to envisage, the simplest to set before ourselves as a goal of achievement). But to safeguard this freedom is far harder. We find, in fact, that the freedom we have talked about is not one thing but many. We discover that, if it is to be preserved, it has to become a positive force—a "freedom for . . ." or a "freedom of . . ." as well as a "freedom from. . . ." We know that, for its preservation, freedom of association is as important as freedom of speech; freedom of assembly is as important as both; freedom from hunger and fear and ignorance, more fundamental still. But we also know that without the Rule of Law underlying and undergirding all the freedoms, there is no freedom at all. Africa is especially vulnerable to criticism here. A newly-independent state is a fragile thing. As events have shown, it is not difficult for a handful of mutineers in the army to threaten its very existence. And, in the attempt to safeguard that existence, it is tempting to disregard or bypass the Rule of Law, to use, for example, preventive detention without access to the courts as a normal procedure, and to defend its use on patriotic grounds.

I am not going to give a lecture on democracy or to make a case for one form of democracy over against another—though this is in fact the debate which is dividing and at the same time involving the whole human race. This is also the debate into which the African continent, more than anywhere else on earth, is being most powerfully drawn. To talk about "nonalignment" is one thing. To achieve it in the modern world, where you are necessarily dependent for so much on outside resources, is quite another. I am not going to argue one way or the other about democratic institutions; I am sure that that argument never ceases!

But I *am* going to point the relevance of the Christian faith to our world; the meaning of the Christian Church for our world. And to ignore the subject of freedom, and of freedom in the widest possible context, would be to ignore the contemporary situation altogether.

But I want to turn from the current discussion about freedom and its forms and to look at freedom *as it is in itself* as part of the human condition. And again, may I first of all disarm the critic who thinks this an academic subject by stating—as clearly as I can and with all the conviction I possess—that freedom is a need implanted in human nature itself. That if I believe this, and if at the same time I believe in God as Creator, as Maker of that human nature, as the mind behind that creation which we call mankind, then freedom is and must be a primary concern to me as a Christian. I cannot be content simply with the bandying about of words; still less with a purely emotional response to the word "freedom" itself. I must go much deeper, and try to discover what freedom is as I know and experience it in my own human life; then to consider it, so far as I am able, against the background of God's plan and purpose for his people; finally to see it specifically in the context of Christianity—of Christ and his Church.

I am not clever enough, or well-educated enough perhaps, to have any kind of original ideas on so tremendous a theme. But even if I were, I know I would have to restrict myself to what I can understand from my own experience and from my observation of the world of men. And even here I need help from those who are wiser and more percipient than I.

"Man is born free," says the philosopher, "and everywhere he is in chains." What is more certainly true is that man, from the moment of his birth, needs and longs for security: the security of his mother's arms; the security of hearth and home; the security of the tribe; the security of the soil from which he gets his life. But, paradoxically, man cannot *remain* secure unless he also ventures forth in search of wider horizons. Watch a small child, how soon he wants to leave his mother's arms and stretch his own legs; expand "his range of activities" and feel "the development of his own powers".[1] However often he fails and is frustrated; however often he is tempted to go back to security and warmth and comfort, he presses on. He must be free! And his freedom—at this stage—consists in learning to use his own limbs, to overcome the challenges of the things that surround him.

But the child soon discovers that he must be free from the control of persons as well as free in the world of things. And, paradoxically again, as soon as the protective, maternal, secure environment is left behind, man "seeks to follow and to emulate the successful pioneer whom he has watched admiringly . . . he seeks to surpass

[1] Dillistone, *The Christian Faith*, pp.32–3.

or to overcome the rival who in any way interferes with his own progress". This is the pattern
of life. This, we may truly say, *is* human history
itself. "Whenever an individual or a society stays
within a well-defined area and moves according
to a well-defined rhythm of existence, history is
scarcely in the making. The regular pattern can
be described—but that is all. History is concerned
with the man who, for no immediately obvious
reason, goes out from the settled and familiar, not
knowing whither he goes. It is concerned with the
band of slaves who, having been stirred to action
by the example of a revolutionary leader, break
loose from their bondage and set out upon their
journey over the trackless desert to the promised
land".[2] There does not appear to be much connec-
tion between the small boy adventuring for the
first time beyond the village boundary and the
astronaut strapping himself into his space-capsule
to reach the moon. But in fact "the basic motiva-
tion is the same"—I quote again—"Since first a
living human being broke through the bounds of
the safe and secure and ventured out into the
unknown, *freedom*, so to speak, has been in the
blood. The urge is there and it cannot be denied".[3]
It is not only, quite simply, a break with the past
or a turning away from the familiar or the con-
quest of those powers which would shut man in.
"It is also a breaking through into the unfamiliar,
and therefore must always see the advent of a new

[2] *idem*.
[3] Dillistone, pp.33–4.

man, a hero, a leader, a deliverer. The 'free man' leads his brothers into freedom . . ." This, surely *is* human life, *is* history itself. And if man is asked why this craving for the far horizon, why this urge for mastery, why this determination to go forward and conquer, he can only say, as we are told the conqueror of Mount Everest said when asked the same question, "Because it is there!"

And so, already, I have indicated two things about freedom which I am certain are true; not just academically proven, but true in experience, in daily life. First, that the need for it is implanted in human nature ineradicably. Secondly, that because it is so, the human community as well as the individual responds to this need. The free man cannot remain alone in his freedom. He must lead his brothers to the horizon, to the undiscovered, to the invincible, and he must win their freedom with his own. And from these two conclusions follows a third—at least for those who believe in a personal Creator—namely, that this truth about human nature and human history is inescapably also a truth about God in his dealings with men. So the record of those dealings, the earliest record that we possess, is shot through with the subject of freedom. We should expect nothing else.

The Hebrew people are a pastoral people. The story of God's chosen family, the family of Abraham, is the story of their life as it is; centring on a quiet round of custom, of family relationships, of the simplicities of village life. And then that dreamer Joseph appears in the story, and all is changed, for he is a man "clearly set in a different mould from that of his brothers, leading them ultimately into strange new conditions where they were to become aliens in a foreign land. The pattern of family conforming is . . . broken." Individual and community, leader and followers begin to move out into new ways.

But with the appearance of Moses the whole process quickens and gathers pace and momentum. Here is one whose whole life, whose whole meaning, is summed up in the imperious words he addresses to Pharaoh: "*Let my people go!*" And the story of that Exodus is from first to last the story of a community—in this case God's community—moving out in search of freedom. But before they begin their quest, we are told, they and their leader are bound to God by the unbreakable bonds of the Passover. And all through their history, all through the centuries, from the moment of the Passing over of the angel of death to the final destruction of their Temple by the Roman armies, they know that their freedom *and their obedience* to God are ONE. It is *this* knowledge which sustains them when they are fighting for their lives under Judges and Kings, from Joshua to David and from David to Judas Maccabaeus. It is this knowledge too, proclaimed to them through the lips of a Jeremiah, an Isaiah, an Ezekiel, which leads them to see in the darkest days of defeat and exile and homelessness a more blazingly glorious vision of the meaning of freedom. For it is then that they recognize—what other race in history had recognized it?—that their enemies are not simply enemies of flesh and blood—the Philistine, the Amalekite, the Assyrian—but their own treasons and treachery; their unfaithfulness to the God who has freed them and led them forth from slavery; their forgetfulness of the covenant binding them to him alone; their whoring with strange gods. For in this story, whatever the actual event may be and whatever the crisis, three elements remain constant:

It is God himself who is the leader—the saviour of his people.

He uses for this purpose of leadership and of salvation always a *human* agent.

The freedom that is sought and won, the process of that seeking and that victory, is a process always linked to a greater or less degree with *suffering*. Moses commanding, exhorting, encouraging his followers in the desert, in the name and with the authority of their God; Moses pleading on behalf of his people because he alone may represent them before their God; Moses broken and almost destroyed by the stubbornness and wilfulness of his people towards God. This is the meaning of freedom and the realization of it as we see it in the Old Testament.

Now look at the New. The *first* public statement of God's purpose: "I am come to preach deliverance to the captives, and the opening of the prison to them that are bound . . ." These are the words with which Christ proclaims the reason for his coming. Freedom! But before he utters them "He was led up of the Spirit into the wilderness . . ."

There was a striking novel by Rose Macaulay which appeared in England soon after the war, called *The World My Wilderness*. Its background and its theme was the devastated, shattered world of London after the bombs had fallen, and of man trying to find himself again in the waste and desolation. In Africa there is another kind of wilderness which is an enemy, in the wild forest and bush which can so swiftly return and over-run all that the toil and sweat of man has achieved. Whether in a city or in a desert man can always find his wilderness; for the wilderness, like the stable, is part of human existence, and—because it is so—is used by God for his own purposes. "He was *led up* of the Spirit *into the wilderness*." That confrontation, then, was begun in *obedience*; not initiated by himself. It was a response, an answer to the call of the Father who had sent him into the world to proclaim a message of freedom to the sons of men.

And it was there, alone in the wilderness, that the battle for freedom was joined. "He was led up of the Spirit into the wilderness to be tempted of the devil", and, we are told, "he was tempted in all things like as we are."

"Turn these stones into bread. . . ." Satisfy your

desires, your passions, your physical longings. Satisfy them, man, because you must show your freedom. They are *your* powers; you were given them by God; they are there for the using! Be free and use them!

"And he took him to a pinnacle of the Temple and said ... 'Throw yourself down.' " Don't be afraid to use your freedom, man, set no limits to the way you use God's world. Nature itself was made for man! Be free—and show your freedom by your contempt! Be free because you are God's creature, not the slave of his creation!

"And he showed him all the kingdoms of the world, in a moment of time .., 'All this I will give you ... if you will fall down for a moment and worship me.' " Yes, man, bow your knee a moment. You are alone in the wilderness. There is none to see! "And then ... all this power will be yours." You want freedom; you have come to proclaim it in your own person; there are millions upon millions waiting to follow you. It is power you need! Power and glory! That is freedom. Come, man, be free!

"And Jesus said, 'It is written thou shalt *worship* the Lord thy God—him only shalt thou serve.' And Satan departed from him for a season." *For a season*.

The wilderness—like the stable—is a place of meeting. The stable, of the meeting of God and Man; the Creator and his creation. The wilderness, of Christ and the Adversary; of God and the devil. But both alike are places which tell us the true meaning of freedom. He who is almighty, all-holy, all-knowing, is wrapped in swaddling clothes and laid in a manger—because by that obedience alone can he identify himself with man and so become man's Saviour. "Jesus, well aware that the Father had entrusted everything to him, and that he had come from God and was going back to God . . . *laid aside his garments . . .*" (John 13:3-4).

He laid aside the garments of his glory and girded himself with the towel of a servant.

He who is almighty, all-holy, all-knowing "is tempted in all points like as we are, yet without sin"—because by *that* obedience, and by that obedience alone can he proclaim liberty to the captives and the opening of the prison to them that are bound.

The Christian faith says this: freedom is not freedom without obedience. Freedom, if you accept the existence of a personal God, of a God who *cares* for the world he has created, must involve obedience to his laws. Not because they are arbitrary; but because they are the very expression of his love.

The perfect example of this freedom, therefore, can only be found in one who is also perfect in his obedience.

Christ can proclaim liberty to the captives and the opening of the prison to them that are bound because he, by his obedience, is wholly free. And it is *this* freedom which he gives to his Church and to each single member of his Church.

It is this freedom which is its power and its glory to the end of time.

4

Sin: Fact or Fantasy?

Perhaps some of you have read Alan Paton's *Cry the Beloved Country*. Although now it is nearly forty years since it was published, and such vast and cataclysmic changes have shaken the African continent that the problems, the situations and the tragedies it speaks of are all too familiar, it is a book that will live. It always seems to me that the crux of it is found in that moment where the young African priest, a Zulu, and his European colleague are talking about the future of South Africa, and the African says: "I have one great fear in my heart . . . that when they [the Europeans] are turned to loving, we shall be turned to hating."

"When they are turned to loving, we shall be turned to hating . . ." It is a description, of course, of an actual situation; of a situation that we can recognize only too clearly. But it is not of that situation that I wish to speak. I have chosen this incident, this moment in a novel about race relations in South Africa, to illustrate a permanent and abiding situation within humanity itself. "They" and "we" . . . "loving" and "hating." All that we recognize as part of our own condition, wherever we are, whoever we are. The present fact of estrangement and separation between persons; the present fact of division and confusion in this our own personality. I am talking about *Sin*. This moment in Alan Paton's story brings out, I think, very clearly, some of the elements which we need to understand if we are to deal with the subject honestly.

And here I have to make three assumptions. In the first place sin (however we name it) is something which we recognize as being common to man.

This truth was brought home to me by a small African boy to whom I had given a lift in my car. He wasn't a Christian, and he was poor. I had given him a few cents for a meal and was saying goodbye to him. Jokingly I said: "Be good! Don't get into trouble!" And he replied, in all seriousness, "I am afraid of sin". Because *we* know so well its power in our own lives we do not find it difficult to recognize its power over others. We can assume that it is there, and that it will be operative if it gets the chance. Further, we know that sin is the great *spoiler*: that, however noble our ideals and however strong our determination to work for those ideals, there is the probability—almost the certainty—that they will be spoilt. And, finally, we recognize that although it is so much a part of the human condition, of man as he is, it is also something which man alone is unable to master; it is so strong and persistent an enemy that he either accepts it and submits to its domination or he must look outside and away from himself for deliverance and safety. Yet although all this is true; although it is easy enough to recognize the *fact* of sin, its universality, its consequences in our individual lives and in our world, a *definition* of it is not easy. I shall use one given in a book by Dr Austin Farrer, *Saving Belief*. He says, "To sin is to do the wrong thing in relation to some person." Obviously no definition can cover every aspect or element of sin. It is altogether too manifold and too elusive for that. But this definition, it seems to me, avoids the main dangers of being wholly negative (sin as a refusal, a turning away, a disobedience) or of being too abstract (sin as a thing-in-itself; pride, anger, lust, gluttony, sloth etc., without a context or a setting). And this definition, it seems to me, is also nearest to that which runs through the scriptures—"to do the wrong thing in relation to some person". In the Old Testament perhaps the clearest example and illustration is David himself. David planning the death of Uriah in battle so that David may have Uriah's wife. The scheming, the willed, deliberate order to Joab: "Set ye Uriah in the forefront of the hottest battle and retire ye from him that he may be smitten and die." The full acceptance of the consequences of his act: "Let not this thing displease thee, for the sword devoureth one as well as another." "And when the mourning was past, David sent and fetched Bathsheba to his house, and she became his wife, and bare him a son." Doing the wrong thing—and knowing that he does it. There is no doubt about that here; no way of excuse for David because of diminished responsibility or psychological disturbance. "But the thing that David had done displeased the Lord." "To do the wrong thing in relation to some person . . ." Not only the person of Uriah, not only the person of Bathsheba, but the person of the Lord. This is sin.

And, in the gospels, there is the same clear definition running through the parable which deals most fully with the same subject, the parable of the Prodigal Son.

"Give me the portion of goods that falleth to me." Give it me now: I want it: it is mine! The assertion of independence and the determination to prove it. Nothing could be more willed or more deliberate. "He took his journey into a far country." To get away from home, the farther the better, and so to make the separation as complete as it could be. "And there wasted his substance with riotous living—spent all he had . . . began to be in want." The meaning of that act described in terms of loneliness and desolation and hunger. And again, when the Prodigal comes to himself: "I will arise and go to my Father and will say unto him, Father I have sinned against heaven and before thee . . ." "To do the wrong thing in relation to some person", and that person the one closest to him, his father; that person the one on whom he utterly depends, his Creator and Lord.

You will notice that the Christian definition of sin assumes one stupendous truth: a truth so stupendous indeed that it is hard for man to grasp, and from which he runs to escape. It is the truth that man's *freedom* is limited and can be utterly destroyed by the use he makes of it. To be free to *choose* between right and wrong, to have this kind of freedom, and *only* this, is in fact to be in bondage. "And the Lord God commands the man, saying, of every tree of the garden thou mayest *freely* eat; but of the tree of the knowledge of good and evil thou shalt *not* eat of it; for in the day that thou eatest thereof thou shalt surely die." Behind the story of Genesis lies the great truth about man's freedom. Man created in the image and likeness of God in order that he may be free to love his Creator. Made capable of knowing God precisely because without such knowledge love is impossible, inconceivable. Made capable of joy—that is to say, of freedom to use creatures for his happiness ("of every tree of the garden thou mayest *freely* eat . . . ") precisely because without such joy man's relationship with the creation would be empty and meaninglesss. The Garden of Eden, the place of innocence, is the picture of freedom as God means it to be. And man has been haunted by this vision all his days. But he refuses to recognize that the price to be paid for this freedom is the price of obedience—"thou shalt not eat of it, for in the day that thou eatest therof thou shalt surely die." "And the serpent said unto the woman, ye shall not surely die . . . *ye shall be as gods.*"

I do not intend to talk about the *origin* of sin here; only the *fact* of sin, and the Christian answer to sin. But however we regard the Genesis story as to the origin of sin, we are bound to notice three points. First, that it is by an act of disobedience, a deliberate misuse of his freedom, that man learns the nature of wrong. Secondly, that this act of disobedience is in fact an act of the will; a real choosing, a conscious movement of the whole personality in the wrong direction. Thirdly, that the consequence of the act is sweat and toil and tears, but also separation, "a far country". "He drove out the man and he placed at the east of the Garden of Eden Cherubims and a flaming sword which turned every way, to keep the way of the tree of life."

Now let us consider the fact of sin as it shows itself to us in our own individual lives.

Our generation is far more conscious of the world as a whole than any preceding generation could possibly have been. In the first place the speed of communication between the farthest points on the earth's surface links us together, whether we like it or not. An event, however local its significance may be, is never nowadays a merely local event. It is known, it is news, it is actually seen or heard by millions within a few seconds of its happening. There are not many villages without a transistor radio. The whole human race is immediately involved in the event, for good or ill. And, because of the closeness and inter-relatedness of all that happens, even a small and apparently insignificant event may have vast consequences. This is a new element in the human situation, and Africa as much as any other continent on earth is inescapably involved in it. "The world is shrinking," we say. But what we really mean is that humanity, mankind, is being forced to recognize its one-ness. Ideas, events, catastrophes, movements, ideologies, conferences, wars—none of these, today, can in fact be localized. Each belongs to the whole of humanity, immediately. In a sense, of course, this has always been true. But in our generation it is known and seen to be true. And yet the strange and paradoxical fact is that, despite this process of unification, despite all that makes for the one-ness of humanity, as we look out on the world it is the *dividedness* rather than the unity which is most obvious. A world divided into rich and poor; into East and West; into white and non-white. Again, perhaps, not new in itself. But undoubtedly new in the fact that each such division is a cause of tension, and sometimes of open conflict. At a moment in history which, one might think, would be a moment full of hope; a moment of glorious achievement; a moment for the harnessing of all human effort for good, there is this bitter sense of frustration and failure. Because at the deepest level of all, the level of human relationship, there is division, separation, a *spoiler* at work. And to this *evil* force and power the Christian gives the name of *sin*. But it is not the name that matters: it is the fact. "To do the wrong thing in relation to some person . . ." In what ways does sin show itself most clearly in our present situation here in Africa? Is it possible to define any of them? I think it is.

1. Africa, like the rest of the world, is already feeling the presence of secularism. This is inevitable, inescapable. And it is foolish and blind of the Christian to pretend otherwise. But what does secularism really mean? As we have already seen, it certainly does not and cannot mean simply what is material. It does not mean—it never has—the opposite of spiritual, the use of things which can be seen or touched or handled as opposed to the things which are invisible. What then does it mean? Or rather, where is secularism dangerous or wrong? Not, surely, in the sense that, as Bishop Newbigin says, "The educational and social services which the Church began are taken over by the state", though this is secularism. Not either because "the old forms of ecclesiastical discipline are no longer accepted. The old village community, centred on the church, gives place to the new town, dominated by the factory", though this too is secularism. This process is going forward relentlessly in every part of the world—not least in Africa. And nothing will halt it. Nor should it be, in itself, a cause for fear. No. The sin, the divisive, spoiling element, in what we call secularism, lies much deeper. It lies in the fact that man the creature is forgetting his true nature. It lies in the face that man, dependent utterly on God, has ceased to adore his Creator. And so is lost, "in a far country".

2. But in this secularized age, just because man has achieved so much, is ready to set out on his venture to conquer space itself, it is his own *power* that has become his idol, the object of his worship: "I am the master of my fate; I am the captain of my soul"—these are no longer simply words but a faith. Technological skill and the discovery it makes possible—this is wholly good. Even at the level where we recognize its greatest dangers, the possibility that a hydrogen bomb war may destroy the world, we can also recognize what this power, harnessed to man's needs, can do for good. It is *not* the power that is wrong. It is the direction of it. It is the refusal to give honour to him who created the power, whose power it truly is. It is, as St Paul said to the Christians in Rome, those long centuries ago, "to change" the glory of the uncorruptible God into an image resembling corruptible man, "to worship", serve, "the creature more than the Creator". This is the sin of pride; the sin of human power.

3. Secularism; power—but also aggressiveness. The conflicts which characterize our modern world, whether they are ideological or racial or nationalist in their origin, all have this mark in common; a determined self-assertion. "Sovereignty", "the surrender of sovereignty" —what do our phrases really mean except a deliberate and willed cleaving to what is *my own*? And, out of this, a greed and a lust for what is *not* my own?

Nationalism in itself is good. It is, after all, the

driving force which creates nations. But nationalism possessed by greed or pride or anger, this is wholly evil, and wholly destructive too. And it is a reality in Africa as potent as anywhere else in the world. And it is sin.

I have deliberately turned your eyes out on the world around you, and tried to express the meaning of sin—as the Christian understands it—in the context of the world and of our own continent and country. And I have done so because I believe the great challenge which the Christian ought to face lies there. We cannot contract out of our world. It is there, *in the market-place*, that the Christian ought to be. Because it was there, in the market-place, that the Master also stood, confronting sin.

"He eats and drinks with publicans and sinners", they said of him. "I am not come to call the righteous, but sinners", he said of himself. Christ goes where sin is, even though he alone can say, "Which of you convicteth me of sin?"

To the market-place, so familiar to us all in Africa. A microcosm of the whole country, attracting to itself every kind of person that society can name: the rich and the poor; the buyer and the seller; the honest man and the crook. It is one of the joys of a safari in Masasi to stop the car at a roadside market and to buy some simple thing like sugar-cane or coconuts. Because, as soon as you stop, the world is crowding round you to find out who you are, where you are from, where you are going. And the questions and the answers reveal so clearly the very nature of mankind. When John Bunyan in his *Pilgrim's Progress* painted the picture of "Vanity Fair" as an image of the world, he was describing what man knows in every market-place, everywhere, through the ages.

And although it is possible to talk about sin in the context of the world as it is, it only becomes meaningful to talk about sin as we know it in the world of our own heart. It is we who are standing there in the market-place also; buying and selling, quarrelling and laughing, living and dying.

Do you remember how Christ went one day to the house of Simon the Pharisee? Simon obviously wanted to see and prove this young prophet for himself. So he made a supper party and invited a few friends of his own sort. It was a success until that woman burst in on them and made that fantastic scene. Going straight to Jesus; kneeling at his feet; weeping; wiping his feet dry with her hair. Naturally he, Simon, had to show his disapproval. A known prostitute. If this man were the prophet they say he is in the market-place he would know what kind of a woman she is. But, "Simon, I have something to say to you ... something about a creditor and his two debtors ... something you will understand very well. One who owes him five hundred, the other fifty. Both forgiven ... " and then the sudden, piercing question, "Which of them will love him most?" "I *suppose* that he to whom he forgave most." "Quite right! Now look at the woman who has caused you such distress. You didn't even give me the normal courtesies of water to wash my feet, of a salutation, of anointing—but she has washed my feet with tears, kissed them ever since I came in, wiped them dry with her hair ... So I say to you, Simon, that her many sins are forgiven, because she loved much. To whom little is forgiven, the same loveth little." And then the comment: "Who is this that forgives sins also?"

What is sin, then? What is it, in its essence, this divisive, frustrating, formidable force? And how is it to be met?

The Pharisee and the Prostitute. To the eyes of those who stand and gossip in the market-place one is the representative of God's law: a lover of righteousness, a teacher, a leader, a power in the land. And the other is just a fallen woman, an outcast, a notorious evil-liver. It is only when both are in the presence of Jesus Christ that their true status is made known. They are *both* sinners. And both acknowledge the *fact* of sin. Simon only too readily acknowledges it in the person of this woman who has invaded the privacy of his home. The woman, by her tears, in her own person as she kneels at the feet of Jesus and tries to express her grief. But it is Jesus himself who shows them the true meaning, the heart of the matter. "To whom little is forgiven, the same loveth little." It is Jesus himself alone who says to the woman "Your sins are forgiven ... go in peace."

What does this mean to us? I want you to forget for the moment incidents in this story and to remember only the words of Christ: "To whom little is forgiven, the same loveth little", for there, if anywhere in the gospels, is the true meaning of sin and forgiveness.

They are astonishing and improbable words. If they do not seem so to us, perhaps it is because they are too familiar; or perhaps it is because we have forgotten the reality of love.

"Sin", we have said, "is to do the wrong thing in relation to some person." And that is as true a definition, perhaps, as we are able to get. But, in fact, sin is only recognizable for what it is, is only capable of forgiveness at all, if it is seen that that person is in fact God himself.

We lie. What does it matter? It was only a small thing, only a slip of the tongue really, only a cover for our own folly and inadequacy. But we do not see the mouth of Christ struck by the mockers. We do not hear the lips of Christ cry "I thirst".

We steal. Only a little matter; a few cents; a few ideas in an exam paper; a few shreds of someone else's reputation. Nothing at all to worry about. And we do not hear the blows of the hammer as the nails go through his hands and into the wood of the Cross.

We fornicate. Well, so does everyone, sooner or later. It is just something inevitable, inescapable. The time will come when we can forget this passion. But not yet. And we do not hear the sound of the whip as it falls, or see the thorns pressed down upon his head.

"They know not what they do." "To whom little is forgiven the same loveth little."

Sin is disobedience. Sin is rebellion and revolt. Sin is exile in a far country, in a land of unlikeness. It is all this. In reality, in itself, sin is a refusal of love. But you can only begin to know this when you begin to know also who love is.

> Love bade me welcome; yet my soul drew back
>> Guilty of dust and sin
> But quick-ey'd love, observing me grow slack
>> From my first entrance in,
> Drew nearer to me, sweetly questioning
>> If I lacked anything.

> "A guest", I answered, "worthy to be here."
>> Love said, "You shall be he."
> "I the unkind, ungrateful? Ah my dear
>> I cannot look on thee."
> Love took my hand, and smiling did reply
>> "Who made the eyes but I?"

> "Truth, Lord, but I have marr'd them; let my shame
>> Go where it doth deserve."
> "And know you not", says Love, "who bore the blame?"
>> "My dear, then I will serve."
> "You must sit down", says Love, "and taste my meat."
>> So I did sit and eat.

GEORGE HERBERT

5

God and Evil

I suppose each of us has had the experience of some sudden, extraordinary shock which is in no way personal, and yet which stays in our memory, so that when we think of it we can still recapture the fear or the horror of it. It is vividly present to us because it is almost part of us. I think there was something of this experience for thousands of people when the news broke that Dag Hammarskjöld's plane had crashed, and that he was dead. It was, you will remember, at a moment of great crisis in the Congo. Everything seemed to turn on the success or failure of the negotiations he was carrying on. It was at that very moment when a vital meeting was to take place that he was killed. As the news came over the radio it was almost as if the world's heart missed a beat. Would there be disaster just when there seemed to be hope? Would there be chaos and horror just when there seemed to be a chance of peace? One small miscalculation, one petty, momentary mistake, and perhaps the security of the whole world was in the balance.

I have used this illustration simply to point to what is there, lying behind the whole tremendous problem of God and Evil. But you can no doubt think of many such moments out of your own experience. The strange thing about such moments is that they bring into such sharp relief the circumstances in which we first encountered them. To me, that plane crash will always be associated with a small mud-and-thatch hut in a village I was visiting. The lamp was lit, I switched on my transistor radio for the news; there was no one to discuss it with when it came over the air— just the shock of hearing it, the sense of utter loss. And somehow this in itself emphasized for me the element of apparent chance, of bad luck operating as it were within the Divine Providence.

As Pierre Teilhard de Chardin says, "How can these diminishments which are altogether without compensation, wherein we see death at its most deathly, become for us a good?"[1] When we stop to consider our world—the actual world we know and see around us; the world of which we form a part—we recognize immediately a colossal paradox. For we see, unmistakably, a world of order. We see times and seasons, sunrise and sunset, seed-time and harvest. And the life we live in this world is inextricably involved with this steady, ordered course, so that nothing we do and nothing we think about lies outside it. Man is a creature who is born, grows to adolescence, to maturity, to old age; and to each part of his life belong certain qualities and capabilities and

[1] *Le Milieu Divin*, p. 67.

characteristics. He can talk about "the laws of nature" simply because (in spite of all the infinite variations and mutations that he discovers) there *is* such a principle of order and purpose in the world he knows. And yet—cutting across this very world of order is this other quality: the quality which shows itself in the sudden calamity and disaster—the catastrophe which seems to make nonsense of it all.

And then, too, this element can be on the grand scale or at the level of the individual. It can show itself in an earthquake, killing thousands, maiming and mutilating thousands more. Or it can show itself in the motor accident, the thalidomide baby, the blind eyes of a child.

It is all this—and so much more—that we mean when we talk about "the problem of evil". But it is, of course, only a *problem* in the truest sense to those who believe that God is, and that he is good. "Is God good? Answer me Yes or No. Is he almighty? Yes or No, please. Would a good person ever let innocence suffer if he could help it? Oh, he wouldn't, wouldn't he? Well then why does God . . ."[2]

I have said that evil is only a problem in the truest sense to those who believe that God is, and that he is good. To others, evil is not a problem, it is just a fact. To the Marxist, for instance, who must believe that all behaviour, all morality, is a consequence of an economic substructure to society

[2] Farrer, *Saving Belief*, p.37.

and that the material universe is all there is, evil is a consequence of the whole dialectical process. To the scientific humanist, evil is something which can be ameliorated or even overcome by man's advancing skill and knowledge; in the meanwhile it must be endured rather than explained. To the simple agnostic, evil, like every other apparently ultimate thing, is inexplicable. To all these, therefore, evil is a fact rather than a problem; a fact rather than a challenge. But to those who believe in a personal God, a God who is also good, to them the presence of evil (however you define it) whether in the vast catastrophic form it can assume or at the level of the person, the individual, is a great and inescapable challenge. Or at least, it ought to be. For who can avoid, at some time or other, having to meet it in his own life? I have given an example of this already in the more general sense of a sudden catastrophe which could affect the lives of millions. But any minister of God is meeting it at the individual and personal level over and over again. I was in a village in my diocese in Tanzania for the sacrament of Confirmation. After the service, as usual, numbers of children crowded round, and the rumour soon got about that I had some footballs to distribute to the schools. Presently a small boy with a very withered "polio" leg hopped out of the crowd on his home-made crutch (without which he could not move at all) and said, "I want a football". A simple and not a particularly extravagant example, I hope. But one which points the problem. How does a good and omnipotent God allow innocent suffering? How does he who is almighty, all-holy, all-knowing, all-loving *care* for a world in which such things happen?

Let me say at once that I am not so presumptuous or so foolish as to imagine that I can give a simple answer to a question which has been argued and debated through all the centuries of Christian history. But at least I can try to re-state some of those fundamental truths without which the problem cannot be faced at all.

The first is that God *is* almighty, omnipotent, all-knowing. "God cannot be God, he cannot differ from us in the essential way which makes us finite and him infinite, unless his mind is infinite too. . . . Properly speaking, there are no problems or difficulties for God. He sees the answer in seeing the question." But because *we* are human creatures, because our minds (however well-stocked, well-educated, well-disciplined) are limited by our very "creatureliness", we can only see (if we dare to look at all) a "vast synthesis of fact, a bewildering balance of competing interests, a mountain of mental labour and an agony of awkward choice, and so *we* see as *difficulty*, what for God is just *multiplicity*." And this truth about the omnipotence of God carries with it another truth: the truth that God stands over against the world he has made, as Creator over against creation; as Providence over against the ordered world; as Goodness over against the good things so created. Dr Farrer has a fine passage in which he writes:

The sun, in the height of a clear noon, radiates on every earthly thing that lies open to his light; and so a transcendent Godhead must radiate on every creature subject to his will. All things are external to his being; *nothing* is outside the sphere of his action. But when we compare God with the sun, it is the utter *unlikeness* of things compared that makes the splendour of the parable. The universal radiation of the sun is the monotonous operation of a physical energy; the inescapable sovereignty of God is a distinct alteration of personal will bestowed upon every existent creature . . . a mind which simultaneously and perfectly attends to all things.[3]

Or, more simply, "Not even a sparrow falls to the ground . . ."

But having said all that, I know that all I have truly said is that the omnipotence and the omniscience of God is a *mystery*. It is a mystery in the deepest sense of the word; a truth so tremendous, a light so brilliant and splendid, that to a created human intellect it is overwhelming—incomprehensible—its very light a blinding darkness; its very truth, in human language at least, inexpressible. And this is, in fact, the meaning and heart of religion itself. This acknowledgement of our creatureliness and our dependence and our need.

[3] Farrer, *Saving Belief*, p. 43.

The problem of evil is real enough to each of us. At some moments in our life it may be so real that it drives out every other consideration. Pain, suffering, desolation may press so hard upon us—either through our own actual experience of them, or because of the involvement of those we love—that there is nothing else we can think of; not even God himself. But this is part of the human condition, part of the truth that we are creatures; creatures made for God. That is the point! The Christian faith asserts that this creation, dependent upon God at every moment of its being, has a purpose, has an *end*—and that that purpose and that end is God himself. It is this alone which gives meaning to the mystery of evil in this present world; the fact that this present world—with all its loveliness and glory, as well as all its ugliness and pain—is only a *part* of God's plan; only the beginning, not the fulfilment. That just as we can get dim glimpses and scattered hints of a love shining through the loveliness of creation; so, in the dark places, we can get hints and glimpses also of a purpose and a meaning far beyond the reach of our own limited intelligence. "When God removes evils in the human sort of way, it is commonly by the employment of human hands", says Dr Farrer again.[4] "His own divine way is to make unthought-of goods out of permitted evils, and to triumph by new creation." What we need, then, is not so much a philosophy which

[4] *Saving Belief*, p. 57.

will explain the problems of evil, as a means, an instrument, a way to meet it in our every-day lives. And it is exactly this that the Christian faith claims to give us.

We have seen, in the course of these addresses, certain things as the symbols of our life: the stable, the wilderness, the market-place. All of them so familiar to us in Africa. But what is more familiar than the roads we use to move about the country? In my diocese of Masasi, I had good reason to think a great deal about roads; for at least half the year the major roads can be impassable: bridges swept away by flooded rivers, an aftermath of mud and rocks; a feeling of uncertainty at the beginning of every journey as to whether one will get to the other end in safety. And yet, how thrilling they can be! What a joy when they are open! This one, that passes close to the Cathedral, leading up from the coast into the heart of Malawi; worn by the feet of slaves and soldiers, of missionaries and merchants, of millions who have just passed by, unknown except to God. And the small tracks which go from village to village—what a history is theirs! The whole history, in a sense, of the men and women and children whose feet have made them; feet carrying messages of joy and sorrow; news of triumph and disaster; feet bearing the bridegroom to the bride, the child to his teacher, the body to its grave.

If the market-place is a symbol for the world and its concerns, the road is a symbol for man and his needs. "After this he went journeying from town to town and village to village, proclaiming the good news of the kingdom of God." That is the description of the first days of the Gospel. The roads and tracks of Galilee and the lakeside; of Judaea and the country round about. And "with him were the Twelve and a number of women who had been set free from evil spirits and infirmities." So it was that they found themselves on the road from Jericho to Jerusalem, "and as he was leaving the town, with his disciples and a large crowd, Bartimaeus . . . a blind beggar, was seated *at the roadside*." So familiar a sight along that hot and dusty road! No doubt Bartimaeus was not the only one sitting there in the dust with his hands stretched out. "Hearing that it was Jesus of Nazareth he began to shout 'Son of David, Jesus, have pity on me'." You can see it all so clearly. The crowd trying to stop his cries; the disciples urging Jesus to hurry past: "If you stop for this one you'll have to stop for all of them—that's the worst of this road, it's full of beggars . . . push on, Master . . . don't listen." But still the cry, "Jesus, Son of David, have mercy on me." *And Jesus stood*. And Jesus stood there by the roadside, with the crowds pushing and thrusting and shouting round him. "What do you want me to do for you?" "Master . . . I want my sight back." "Go. Your faith has cured you." "And at once he recovered his sight and followed him on the road." *Jesus stood*! Jesus the Son of God stood—for one blind beggar in the dust.

It is true that Christians should be ready to

think about and to give reasons for their faith. And in our modern world there is a special importance attaching to a really intelligent and honest appraisal of the difficulties of faith. Certainly in a university there is no excuse for the Christian who is prepared to use his intelligence in every field except religion; to justify his refusal on the ground that his faith and his reason exist in separate compartments. To abdicate intellectual responsibility and effort in this way is cowardice rather than prudence. But it is equally true that, in dealing with the problem of evil—the problem, that is, of catastrophe and disaster as it touches human life in this world—what we need is not a philosophy, but a weapon. And that weapon is prayer.

What is prayer—in its essence? "A blind beggar, seated at the roadside." You cannot find a better picture of man's attitude to God in prayer than that. For we *are* blind in so many ways. Blind in the sense that, as creatures, we have not the power to see through to the heart of the mystery of the Godhead. Our very nature as creatures, our limitedness and littleness and dependence, throws us back on ourselves. We have not, and we cannot have, the capacity to comprehend the incomprehensible; to grasp the infinite. We are blind before the greatness of the mystery itself. But we are also blind before its *glory*! God's will, God's touch upon his creation is always glorious—even when to us it appears as pain and suffering and defeat. We have not here, sitting by the roadside in the dust, the capability of distinguishing the sounds, the footsteps, the ebb and flow of voices which pass us by. Above all we are blind to the immediate moment of loss or frustration or misery as it affects us here and now. The world closes in around us, and when we cry out all that we get back is a negative, a refusal: "Be quiet . . . you're not the only one . . . stay where you are, in the dust." And the roadside is the place for beggars, certainly. Let us face the fact that the very heart of prayer lies here: we are beggars, suppliants—ways that. Because that is the very meaning of creatureliness. Perhaps what the modern world needs most of all to rediscover is the truth about creation. It is because man has forgotten that he is a creature, dependent at every moment on his creator, that he can so easily misuse creation itself. Always we are beggars, not because through our own fault we have misused our lives, our gifts and talents (though we may have!), but because life itself and all that goes with it; all the glory of it; all the power of it; every "many-splendour'd thing" is a free gift from the God who made us. We are beggars, and we are blind. But Jesus of Nazareth passes by along that road. We cry, "Son of David, Jesus, have pity on me", "Have mercy on me, Jesus, Son of David". "*And Jesus stood.*" If one part of the meaning of prayer is expressed so perfectly in the figure of Bartimaeus by the roadside, the other is shown more perfectly still in these words: Jesus stood. Jesus, the Son of God; almighty, all-holy, all-knowing, all-loving—this

71

one who is from all eternity—"stood", there in the dust. "What do you want me to do for you?"

What is prayer really? We like to think of it, particularly when we are in trouble or when our needs loom large, as a violent tremendous effort of the will; a beating on the heavens with all the strength we possess. We like to think of it—for the most part—as that activity which will some-how bend God's will, or at least his attention, in our direction only, immediately. We like to exclude from it, only too often, the elements of praise and adoration, of penitence and thanksgiving which run through the Psalms of David, the liturgy of the Church. These parts of prayer are all right for public use, no doubt. But for myself, alone, it is different. But what is prayer?

"Behold, I stand at the door and knock. If any man hear my voice, and open the door, I will come in to him and will sup with him, and he with me." Prayer is not simply man, his hands out-stretched, his voice crying out from the roadside. It is also Jesus, the Son of God, standing, knocking, waiting to come in.

6

Why the Cross?

One of the advantages of staying in a university is the chance it gives of being involved in its activities. Only this morning, one of the lecturers in the Fine Arts department used me as a model for some sculpture. Whilst he was wrestling with the unwilling clay he turned to me and said, "Sometimes I think that ears are more trouble than they're worth." I saw what he meant! But as I was considering how to approach the subject for this address, that incident and those words seemed somewhat to the point. The artist, struggling to create something beautiful, is involved with inanimate clay. The Creator himself is involved with sentient, living, wilful humanity. And this humanity is somehow separated from him, whilst needing above all else union with him for which it was created. "From first to last this has been the *work* of God. He has reconciled us men to himself through Christ, and he has enlisted us in this service of reconciliation. What I mean is, that God was in Christ reconciling the world to himself." So St Paul. And it is a full and complete statement of what the Christian faith claims to be. A work of God. In Christ. And that work, a reconciliation between the world and himself. So we are going to consider more carefully the meaning of this work; the means by which it is accomplished; our own part in it.

In my last address we were at the roadside, outside Jericho. The roadside, which is the place where man in his blindness and in his poverty sits in the dust. The roadside, which is also the place where man discovers the meaning of life again. "What do you want me to do for you?" "Master, I want my sight back." "Go, your faith has cured you." Last night, the roadside; but tonight, a hill outside the city. The place of execution. They call it The Skull.

I think the road is easier to understand than the hill—certainly easier than the hill called Golgotha. The Christ who "goes about doing good"—healing the sick, bringing sight to the blind and hearing to the deaf, recovering hope for the despairing and the lost; the Christ who says "Come unto me all ye that labour and are heavy-laden and I will refresh you", the Christ who is not afraid to talk with publicans and sinners or to rebuke the Scribe and the Pharisee. This Christ, whether he walks the road of Galilee or of Africa, is one that I must hear, must follow. For in the world there is so much pain that needs healing; so much sorrow that needs comfort; so much loneliness that needs love. Is not this alone a work of reconciliation? Is not this alone, perhaps, God's work in Christ? Certainly, all through the ages, there have been those who have tried to make of Christianity a religion which would concern itself with these things and nothing more. But they have been defeated and thrown back by two harsh facts; a gallows, and an empty tomb. Eliminate either of these (and because they stand so close together they are as one—"now at the place where he had been crucified there was a garden . . . ") and you tear the heart out of the Christian Gospel. Eliminate the Cross, and there is no power! Eliminate the Empty Tomb, and there is no glory!

Let us look fearlessly at the Cross.

You may remember—if you read history or even historical plays—that incident when Joan of Arc was being burnt at the stake. As the flames began to lick her body a soldier pulled a stick out of the fire, broke it, made a rough cross out of it and held it before her eyes till they could see it no longer. To her that rough cross was real—infinitely more real than the silver and gold crucifix on the high altar, no doubt; or the pectoral cross on the bishop's breast. It was real because, although it was only a symbol, she knew as she looked at it the pain and grief and loneliness of death. And so, of course, have all the Christian saints and martyrs through the ages.

But our difficulty, as twentieth-century Christians, in thinking about the reality of the Cross, is that for the vast majority of us it remains an external symbol. We see it every day on the outside of our churches or our hymn books. We use it constantly as a badge or emblem of our denominational allegiance. It has become, inevitably, formalized, part of the institutional organization of Christendom. Yet, at the same time, it has become from time to time unreal in an even more dangerous way—by reason of the sentimentality which can and does surround it in so many of the hymns we sing and the words we use about it. Like the stable and the manger on a Christmas card, the Cross is so often beautified, glamorized into something which it could never be.

So, first of all let us go back to the Hill of the Skull, and consider the cross that stands there against the sky, and ask ourselves quite simply what it means; not, for the moment, what it means in terms of Christian faith and devotion; not, for the moment, what it has *come* to mean on this side of the Resurrection; but what it means *in itself*, there on Golgotha nineteen hundred years ago.

And we cannot fail to remember that it is part of the whole apparatus of Roman law. Of that very thing, in fact, which is reckoned to be Rome's greatest contribution to Western civilization: *Justice*: crucifixion. The killing of a man by the state is the ultimate penalty for a crime against the state, the final satisfaction *in law* that can be exacted of an offender. The cross there on the hill is certainly—to the onlookers for whose benefit it is placed there—a symbol of justice. But it is also, and inescapably, the instrument of *power*: of the power of the state to dispose of the individual not merely by ordering, moulding, shaping his life; but by taking it away. "Don't you know," says

Pilate "that I have *power* to crucify you and have *power* to release you?" And the very fact that the cross is set there, high on a hill, is that it may be a sign to all men everywhere as to where final authority, final power rests.

To Rome it is the sign and instrument of power. To the people it is the sign and instrument of degradation. Crucifixion is, and is meant to be, a stripping away of human dignity. It involves the condemned man in a public spectacle of shame. There is no attempt at concealing either the pain or the defeat of the individual. He is made to carry his own gallows through the crowd. He is stripped naked in the public gaze. He is pinioned and nailed and raised from the ground whilst his fellow men look on. And, for hours, maybe, he hears their mockery as they stand or pass by. The purpose of this kind of execution is that death should be slow in coming, a horrible deterrent to those who see it: a prolonged agony to those who suffer it. It serves therefore a double purpose. The cross is not only an instrument of death, it is also an instrument of utter ignominy and degradation to the spirit of man.

But—these on the hill outside Jerusalem, David's city, the Holy City—it has yet another significance. "They took him *out* to crucify him." *Out*. Outside the city, because "cursed is he that hangs on a tree". The cross is not simply the instrument of power, not simply the means of degrading the human spirit. It is also a symbol of *rejection*. He who hangs there is cursed, is cut off, is driven out and away from the people of God. They must not touch him—let the Gentiles be the executioners. They must not leave his body in sight on the Sabbath—let it be removed and taken right away. He who dies on a cross cannot be part of the Israel of God, for God himself has rejected him.

Power. Degradation. Rejection. Inescapably this was the meaning of the cross to Roman, to man, to the people of God.

And so, surely, the Cross reflects back to us, as we climb that hill to look at it, the very world in which we live ourselves, today; the world of Africa, as much as anywhere else. We are all caught up into the conflict of power—whether we wish it or not. Not merely in its narrower and more obvious sense of a conflict between two rival and mighty power blocs now tearing the world apart. At an even deeper level than that the world is obsessed with the idea of power; with the idea not merely of sovereignty over this or that part of the earth's surface, but of power in itself and the sources of power. Whether those sources lie in the harnessing of waters or the control of oil or the mastering of atomic energy, man must have power. And to have it, he is prepared to degrade, to dehumanize and depersonalize his fellow men. In the name of some ideology or racial ideal he will deny human dignity. In the name of some economic necessity, some hidden law or force, he will maintain a situation in which millions cannot be fully men because they are too hungry. Sometimes, perhaps most often, this degradation is not deliberate; it is simply accepted as irremediable. The world is divided into rich and poor. What can be done about it? And it is a world, certainly, in which an ever-increasing number of men and women feel themselves rejected; cast off by their own society, their own family. Is not this one of the very consequences of urbanization—the up-rooting and the breaking down of the old ties of family and clan and tribe? What is the number of homeless and stateless persons in the refugee camps of Africa and of the world today? How is it that, in Western civilization at least, the problem of the old and the lonely is greater than ever before?

These same stresses and hostilities which divide society, divide our own souls. "What causes wars, and what causes fighting among you? Is it not your passions that are at war in your members?" The power and the glory which nations fight for are also the spur and stimulus of each man's inner pride. The degradation and dehumanization which so characterizes man's dealings with his fellow men at the national level is there, unmistakably, in our own bitter jealousies and resentments and anger. The rejection is there too. The rejection which we allow in our most secret heart by the refusal to love and care. This is the human condition. It is a condition of *estrangement*. And "the estrangement from which we suffer and which threatens to destroy us is not merely among or between men; it is within man . . . our individual inner conflicts, on the one hand, and all the separations and enmities between neighbours and nations, on the other, are facets of an even deeper estrangement; man's separation from his true home, his alienation from the ground and source of his being, his ultimate loneliness and 'lostness', his estrangement from God."[1] This estrangement is what the Church calls sin. "Man is estranged from God and therefore divided against himself. This is his 'fallenness', his 'brokenness', his wretchedness, his hopelessness, his desperate fatal sickness. The recovery of his health," so the Christian Church proclaims, "of his own inner wholeness, depends upon his being restored to his true relation to his Creator, upon his being brought home again. Salvation is reconciliation, at-onement."[2]

"God was in Christ reconciling the world to himself"—from the moment of that birth at Bethlehem where the shepherds ran to greet him, through the long days of childhood at Nazareth, at the river with John, in the wilderness with Satan, in the market-place and at the roadside: "God in Christ reconciling the world to himself." At every moment and in every place this is true, this is Gospel truth. But supremely, and most certainly of all, is it true there on the hill, outside the city. The hill is the place of reconciliation and atonement. The hill is the place where man's long

[1] John Knox, *The Church and the Reality of Christ*, Collins, p. 103.
[2] *idem*.

estrangement is in fact ended once and for all. It is true that the hill is the place of the Passion: of passivity in the sense of complete and absolute obedience, perfect in itself. Yet the hill is also the place of activity: of an action which finally and for ever achieves its purpose. But *only*, of course, if the figure hanging there on the cross against a darkening sky is truly God as well as truly man. For this estrangement and separation is too vast a thing to be bridged by any except God himself.

I remember, as a child, being fascinated by a painting which hung near my bed. It was a famous painting in its day, and it showed a man standing alone in a blizzard, obviously struggling painfully and blindly forward into the teeth of the gale. Behind him, in the picture, was the dim outline of a tent. And the caption read "A very gallant gentleman". It was, in fact, a picture of a certain Captain Oates—a member of the Antarctic expedition led by Scott to the South Pole, and which never returned. And the incident was true. Four members of the expedition had survived the return journey through appalling conditions to within a few miles of base. All were desperately sick men, with Oates, the sickest. In order to give his companions a chance to go forward without having to look after him, he walked out alone into the blizzard to die. "Very gallant" indeed. An example, amongst thousands in every age and in every country of a man giving his life for his friends. An example, certainly, of stupendous courage and love. But still—only an example, only an inspiration. An act which has not, and cannot have, any direct contact with *me*; which may—or may not—move me to admiration. But which cannot save me, because he has no power to save.

From *this* estrangement there is, there can be, no rescuer, no saviour but he who is eternal, changeless and infinite love: he upon whom the whole universe depends for its existence and its essential being: he who, because he is its Creator, can alone be wholly identified with his creation, yet always separate from it. The Hill of Calvary is the place of reconciliation. What happened there, and how was the reconciliation effected? How was this at-onement finally accomplished?

Perhaps the most striking thing about the gospels, and the clearest proof of their integrity, is their failure to add anything to the simple facts which make up the story of the Crucifixion. Although every gospel relates some specially significant detail remembered and told, obviously, by an eye witness of the event, there is no attempt to say, "And this, this particular way of death *is* the reconciliation". Even though the evangelists interpret the words of Jesus, the actions of Judas and the High Priests, of Pilate and the soldiers, of the disciples and the women, in terms of Messianic prophecy and fulfilment, they do not say at any point: "Here is at-onement because there is no other explanation possible." They leave to the Church—to you and me—the events and, above all, the words of the Cross. The truth of the mystery of reconciliation, the meaning of atonement will be revealed, within the Church, to each generation afresh by the power of the Spirit of truth.

History has shown that any attempt to say of this mystery, "Here in this theory alone is the full and final truth" (let us say, for example, the theory of "penal substitution") not only fails to convince or persuade men's hearts; it hardens them and separates them.

What, then, must we do? Are the words of the hymn sufficient?

> *We do not know, we cannot tell,*
> *What pains he had to bear,*
> *We only know it was for us*
> *he hung and suffered there?.*

No. For we have his own words, and they indeed are enough. We stand, then, on the hill of Calvary. And there on the cross above us is the God of Gods, the Lord of Lords. He has come into a world where man's use of power to separate and divide, and if necessary to destroy, is taken for granted. And he meets that power, focused in the instrument of Roman law and sovereignty, with his arms stretched out and pinioned, and the nails driving through his feet: "Father forgive them, they do not know what they are doing."

He has come into a world where man is degraded by his fellow men. And he meets their degradation in its completest form in the nakedness, the stripping, the mockery of the hill—and, aware that all had now come to its appointed end, said, "I thirst". "I thirst"—not just with this parching, agonizing bodily thirst which is the harbinger of death. But, I thirst for the love of man—of all men, everywhere, to the end of time. He has come into a world where men reject and cast out one another. And he meets this rejection at the very point when it can be known and felt most piercingly, outside the city, on the bleak loneliness of the hill known as the Skull.

"At midday darkness fell over the whole land . . . and . . . Jesus cried aloud . . . My God, My God, *Why* hast thou forsaken me?"

"My God, My God, *Why* . . .?" Making the darkness his own. The darkness of rejection. The darkness which is the consequence of man's own turning away from God. "He who knew no sin became sin for us." There is no darkness comparable to that. And he enters into it, he shares it, he identifies himself with it utterly.

Power. Degradation. Rejection: taken hold of, possessed, and utterly transformed by Love eternal. This is reconciliation. This is at-onement. But it is also victory. "It is finished!" "It is accomplished." "I have finished the work which you gave me to do." Man's enemies are defeated and are in rout: *it is for man to make the victory his own.* It is accomplished!

"God . . . in Christ reconciling the world to himself", and the hill of Calvary is the place, the crux of that reconciling act. Yes! but I was not there! It happened so long ago, and in circumstances so different from mine. It is so distant not only in place and time but in *relevance* to ordinary daily life in Africa, here in this exciting world which presses in upon me. Here is the hill called Golgotha, and here is this hill outside Kampala. How are they linked? How do I share in the reconciliation and the at-onement? For "this reconciliation implies a new existence. This is true of reconciliation even in its simplest form, that between two persons. Reconciliation ... is not an abstract relation between two separate individuals; it is the existence of a third entity, real and concrete, in which both share and by which each is to an extent, remade.... But if this is true of reconciliation between two individuals, how much more obviously true it is of ... the total and ultimate reconciliation, involving God and man, our neighbours and our hearts, and indeed 'all things in heaven and on earth'!"[3] Such reconciliation means the coming into being of a new objective order of relationships, a new "body"—a body more inclusive, more enduring, and more significant than any of the other "bodies" to which we may belong. It is just this body, which, according to the Gospel, God acted to create in Christ.

Without the Cross, reconciliation is impossible; without the Church, which is the Body of Christ, reconciliation is meaningless.

The Cross on the hill is the pledge and the

[3] Knox, p. 104.

sign of "God *in Christ* reconciling the world to himself". But it is also the pledge and sign of a new creation. "In Christ" again "all will be brought to life".

If Christianity had stopped at Calvary it would be meaningless. But, "Now at the place where he had been crucified there was a garden . . . "

7

The Lord of Life

"Now at the place where he had been crucified there was a garden . . . ." The Cross is both the instrument and the symbol of power: power used by states and rulers to control, and if necessary to destroy, the individual. The Cross is also, as we have seen, the instrument and symbol of degradation and rejection: the de-personalizing of the person, the casting-out from society of the individual. And all this together means estrangement. So it was at this point, the cross on the hill of Golgotha, that God in Christ completed his work of reconciliation. "It is finished", rang out that voice in the darkness. The work is done! But: "at the place where he had been crucified there was a *garden*." At first sight what an extraordinary and apparently trivial detail to notice. That the hill, the place of the Skull, which represented so much of human cruelty, of human despair, of human futility; the place, after all, of death in its least heroic form; that this hill should stand close by a garden. For, whatever else a garden signifies (and I suppose to an Englishman it signifies perhaps too much!) it signifies life; and life in a very specially rich and meaningful sense. In fact, the idea of resurrection is not an unfamiliar idea at any level except the human. The natural world speaks of it with every winter and every spring that passes. Though perhaps not so clearly in the urbanized, technological world of the West as it once did. I spent over twelve years of my life in a different part of Africa before I came to Tanzania; in fact in the largest African city on the continent—Johannesburg. A city with over a million citizens, more than half of them Africans drawn from every tribe in southern Africa. And most of those that I knew and lived with and loved had been bred, if not born, in the city. The children who learnt in our schools, the young teachers who taught them, the nurses who cared for the sick—these knew virtually nothing of the country in which their grandparents, and perhaps their parents, still lived. And although it is possible to make too much of the theme that runs through, for instance, Alan Paton's *Cry the Beloved Country*—the theme of the simple, unsophisticated, country man bewildered and lost in the great city—although it is possible also to over-emphasize and to bring into disproportion the complexities of urban life contrasted with the simplicities of the village, at least certain facts are true and real.

One of them was brought home to me very soon after I went to live as a priest in Sophiatown. It was the fact that most of the children (and sometimes the whole of Sophiatown seemed to be children) were hungry. Not just hungry in the way that any child is always hungry; but ill with hunger, the hospitals and clinics crowded with cases of malnutrition. And this in the "City of Gold", in the richest city on the African continent. There were reasons, of course. And no doubt you know most of the reasons as well as, or better than, I do. Political reasons, economic reasons, "apartheid" in its worst and most horrible form—the deliberate attempt to push out of sight and so out of mind a vast multitude of one's fellow men. But the point I am trying to make here is a simpler one, and a totally non-controversial, non-political one. In order to do something about that child-hunger; to destroy the destroyer who was at work day and night in our families, killing perhaps a third of the children born there, I had to find food. And in a city—any city—there is only one way of doing that: you have to *buy* it. It does not grow, because you cannot plant seed in concrete, you cannot herd cattle in a busy street, and there is no harvest to be gathered in from paving stones or off refuse-dumps or street lamps. Of course there is a problem of hunger—of hungry children, let me say—in a rural area like that in which the diocese of Masasi is placed. And I am not so foolish or presumptuous as to dwell on the problem to an audience like this. Every new country in Africa is facing the issue of development. There are thousands of peasant-farming areas with subsistence-level farms and *shambas* all over the continent, confronted with almost identical problems. How to improve communications; how to break through the old pattern; how to conserve water; how to encourage better methods. It is, at the human level, the greatest and most exciting challenge confronting us in Africa today. And anyone called to play a part in meeting the challenge is blessed beyond measure. For what it amounts to—this challenge of hunger—is fundamentally one thing only; a recognition that the right use of the land, of the soil and the water and the seed means *life*. And every time I went on safari through our villages, and saw a lot of land being stumped and cleared; here a fine crop of rice; here, in church, an offering of grain, I saw, what in the city could not be seen, what was totally obscured and hidden, something of infinite significance and meaning in those oddly irrelevant words: " . . . at the place where he had been crucified *there was a garden* "—for a garden, above all, is a place of life.

Every great philosophy, every great religion is concerned, of course, with the meaning of life. Either with the way in which man, as man, can come to terms with his environment; take it up and use it to enrich himself physically, mentally and spiritually. Or with the end—the final purpose—of life, how he may best prepare himself for this; viewing the present always in terms of the future, of the ultimate. Man's behaviour is determined by the view he holds of the meaning and purpose of life. It is life which is central to all his thinking, all his hopes and fears. And so the great religious systems of history try to give an answer to this, the central and fundamental question. As the great French philosopher Maritain has said: "The spectacle offered in a general way by the ancient world, the world before Christ, is what might be called the *competition of wisdoms*."[1] And these wisdoms are concerned with the same basic need. There is the wisdom of India and the East, a wisdom primarily and essentially "of deliverance and salvation"; "bound up", as Maritain says, "with a practical science of spiritual perfection and sanctity." Nature must somehow transcend itself, get free from all illusion, break free of all the constraints of cause and effect—to a kind of total emptiness in which the soul can experience truly and "intuitively the existence of the self". A truly noble upward striving of the human spirit is seen as the main object of life, as its highest expression, perhaps, in finding something—nirvana—"that was closer and closer to pure negation".

Then there is Greek wisdom, the wisdom which has so pervaded and filled what is known today as Western civilization. "A wisdom of man, a wisdom of reason . . . turned towards created things and the knowledge of the cosmos, not towards salvation or saintliness or eternal deliverance." A life-affirming wisdom, if ever there was one; provided that you limit the word "life" to what is observable here, all around you: "things, tangible and visible reality". It is the foundation, of course,

[1] Jacques Maritain, *Moral Philosophy*, p. 71.

of all scientific method; of all that we recognize as a condition of advancing knowledge in the modern world.

Finally there is a third wisdom, Hebraic wisdom, the wisdom of the Old Testament. It is not a human wisdom like Greek wisdom. "It is a wisdom", as Maritain goes on to say, "of salvation and of saintliness, of deliverance and freedom, of eternal life." But for it, unlike Hindu wisdom, man does not rise by his own efforts. "It is not in heaven, that thou shouldest say who shall go up for us to heaven, and bring it unto us, that we may hear it and do it . . . ?" "The long unflagging Jewish impatience beseeches God to give himself, a God who wants only to give himself, but who hides himself."[2]

Eastern, Greek, Jewish: these are the three competing wisdoms; each at its highest and best expressing profundities of the human spirit in its search for the meaning of life. Each, moreover, used of God, "the real light which enlightens every man", to enrich and give deeper content to that meaning.

But only the Christian religion places at the heart and centre of this search not an idea, but an event; not a condition or state of being, but a community; not an end to be striven for, but a person to be known and loved. It is Christ who says, not: "Here is life; come and get it", but: "I *am* the resurrection and the life." And it is in the

[2] Maritain, p. 73.

garden, near to the place where he was crucified, that his meaning is made plain; and with it, for his followers, the meaning of life itself.

"I believe", says the Christian, "in the resurrection of the body." A very different thing from saying "I believe in the immortality of the soul", even though "the life everlasting"—also an article of the Christian faith—involves this.

But I believe in the resurrection of the body not as an idea which I have arrived at by reasoning or intuition or inspiration, but as being inextricably linked to an event. "If there be no resurrection," says St Paul, "then Christ was not raised; and if Christ was not raised then our Gospel is null and void, and so is your faith."

What is it in fact that Peter has to say to that vast crowd in Jerusalem "drawn from every nation under heaven" on the first Pentecost of all? What is the heart and core of the good news that he stands there to proclaim? It is very simple. "Men of Israel listen to me; I speak of Jesus of Nazareth, a man singled out by God and made known to you through miracles, portents and signs, which God worked among you through him, as you well know. When he had been given up to you, by the deliberate work and plan of God, you used heathen men to crucify and kill him. But God *raised him to life again*, setting him free from the pangs of death, because it could not be that death should keep him in its grip." "Jesus—the person that you know; whom you have seen here in this very city. Jesus—the person that you know; whose hands have so often healed the sick, given sight to the blind, hearing to the deaf. Jesus—the person that you know; who was handed over to the power of Rome and crucified out there on the hill. This same Jesus is risen from the tomb; is alive and we have seen and heard and touched him!"

This—not just in Jerusalem at Pentecost, but in every city and village where Peter or Paul or Barnabas or James went preaching—this alone was the message; the good news; the Gospel: Jesus Christ; crucified and risen.

But when we come to proclaim this truth, how are we to proclaim it urgently enough? It sometimes seems almost impossible to convey even a fraction of the wonder, of the glory of it. For even though we know it and live by it as the truth which alone makes meaning of our lives, we live with something which has become too familiar. The resurrection, like the Cross, can become an empty symbol. And, unlike the Cross, it is impossible even to imagine it. Impossible, for the witnesses did not witness the resurrection; what they witnessed was an empty tomb with grave-clothes lying in the shape of the corpse they had enclosed. The act, the moment when the body broke through and was set free was a moment not witnessed at all by human sight. How then came this stupendous certainty about the fact? What was it, in those hours after the dawn broke upon the women at the tomb; in those few days when first the message, "He is risen", and then the real presence came to one, to two, to twelve—now here on the road to Emmaus, now there by the lakeside, now in the bolted and bared room where they gathered in fear? What was it which gave the absoluteness of their belief its continuing and unshakeable power? So that, years afterwards, Paul could write, "If Christ was not raised then our Gospel is null and void, and so is your faith"?

I think we can identify three things; three elements which belong to that moment of recognition in the case of each individual appearance of the risen Christ. First, that it is the *same* Jesus. "It is the Lord!" cries John. "Did we not feel our hearts on fire as he talked with us on the road", say Cleopas and his companion. "Lord," says Peter, "you know everything, you know I love you." The resurrection, breaking and sundering and destroying all known categories of human experience, yet leaves him the same person; cognisant of the past—of every little triviality in it, like baking fresh fish on the coals by the lakeside; marked by the past—in hands and feet and side and, dare we think, in the eyes which look upon Peter? Carrying the past with him, so to speak, and therefore being inescapably familiar in every movement and gesture and tone. And yet— "glorious". That is the only adjective which fits him now. "God who raised him from the dead and gave him glory." It is the glory which, so to speak, catches up and holds their gaze, even though, even because, they gaze at him whom they know.

It is the *same* Jesus; but his presence with them conveys its own absolute authority and power. It is this presence, this alone, that brings the certainty. No need for explanation. No need for reassurance as to the *manner* of his breaking the bonds of death. No need for anything, even when confronted with the doubts of a Thomas. "My Lord and My God." It is the same Jesus; and yet, in the glory of his risen body, his authority extends not simply to a part of them—(the best part, perhaps, but still fickle and frail and ready to rebel)—but to the whole of them; without reserve. In the risen Lord they recognize that he who has shown his authority over the power of death—"the last enemy"—has authority also over the whole of life. And this, too, is glory.

Identity; authority—yes, but also and supremely communion: "union with" each and every one to whom he comes. "The God of all grace, who called you *into his eternal glory in Christ*, with himself, after your brief suffering, restore, establish and strengthen you as a firm foundation." This is what they recognize—Mary and Cleopas and John and the others—as he shows himself to them after his resurrection. That the glory which belongs to him, and has belonged to him from all eternity, is a glory they can share. No. Not a glory they *can* share, but a glory that they must share because they are "*in Christ*". And who knew this better than the man setting out on the Damascus road, with his orders to arrest, to destroy utterly these traitors to the truth of God, where he too was overwhelmed by the glory and knew that he was a prisoner of Jesus Christ for ever?

John Knox has said: "To share in the substance of the Church's life is to know the concrete meaning of the Resurrection. To affirm the Resurrection is to affirm the distinctive character of the Church's own existence."[3] The Church came into conscious being when Jesus, alive and exalted after his suffering and death, was made known to those who remembered him—Easter and Whit Sunday do not celebrate two moments, but one only—the moment when those who remembered Jesus became the community in which he was known as present and living spirit. To belong to this community is "to know him and the power of his resurrection".

If we Christians fail to express this knowledge effectively, fail to show this power in our own lives convincingly, it is because of our own impoverished and feeble grasp of the glory which is there surrounding and enfolding us. It is not because the glory itself is dim or faded.

And, all through the history of the Christian Church there are proofs of this; proofs of the glory which shines through even the weakest and the frailest member of that Body. As it happens I was preparing this address on a day which, in Tanzania, is kept as the feast of the African martyrs. And my thoughts turned to one of these, a young girl called Manche Masemola who lived in Sekhukhuniland in the northern part of South Africa some thirty-five years ago. It is a part I

[3] Knox, *The Church and the Reality of Christ*, p. 67.

knew rather well, for my Community had work there and I used to go and visit them. Wild and lovely country: a very small Christian Church compared to the great mass of the population, and even smaller when Manche lived there. But she heard the Gospel from the lips of an African priest, and asked to hear more. She was about fifteen when she became a catechumen; and her parents were bitterly resentful of her doing so. They forbade her to attend classes; beat her cruelly when she disobeyed them. But she longed for the sacrament of baptism, and could not turn back. So she persisted. Until the day when parents and others of her clan took her out to a lonely spot and killed her; so that she was baptized, after all, but in her own blood. "By baptism we were buried with him and lay dead," says St Paul, "in order that, as Christ was raised from the dead in the splendour of the Father, so also we might set our feet upon the new path of life." When we are unable, through our "earthiness" or our coldness or just, simply, our over-familiarity with the mysteries of God, to proclaim them to the world, he raises up his witnesses. All down the ages; in every country and from every race, these "martyrs" (witnesses) appear, to recover for us the wonder of the meaning of his resurrection. But also to remind us that if we want "to know him and the power of his resurrection" it is within his own community that we shall do so. And baptism—Christening—is the door.

"Now at the place where he had been crucified

there was a garden." The place of death: the place of life. The hill: the garden. And it was to the garden that Mary Magdalene came "while it was still dark", and "stood at the tomb outside, weeping". And when Jesus said to her, "Why are you weeping? Who is it you are looking for?", she thought it was the gardener. "If it is you, Sir, who removed him, tell me where you have laid him and I will take him away." Jesus said, "Mary". She turned to him and said *Rabbuni*—my Master.

It is all there, in those few sentences from the pen of John, the friend of Jesus. We need no more, if we are to understand the glory of the living Lord.

We go to find him. But he finds us.

We go in perplexity and sorrow and tears, so that we cannot recognize him. But he is the gardener, and he knows us. But it is not until he calls me by my name: "Mary", the one unique person; the one uniquely *sinful* person, if you like; but, "Mary"—that I see that it is myself, no one else, that he is concerned with. And then I must turn and clasp those glorious feet and say: "My Master!"

8

The People of God

We have been thinking of the meaning of the mysteries of the Christian faith against a background which is familiar to us all. As familiar in Africa today as it was in Israel two thousand years ago. The stable, the wilderness, the market-place, the roadside, the hill and the garden: all are part of our own experience. Each can make known to us in its own way *the power and the glory of God*.

So it is fitting that we should return to the most familiar point of all; in fact that we should return home. And the very word "home" creates for each individual his own unique and special picture. It is a picture not merely of the place, but of the people; not just (perhaps least of all) of the house, the building, but of the family; not just of the known paths and streams and wells, but of the relationship with others—"her sights and sounds, dreams happy as her day, and laughter learnt of friends, and gentleness". This is home. And it is in this sense that I, as a Christian, want to speak about home; home which is, to the Christian, the Church, the family, the people of God. But where can I begin?

The trouble about speaking of what is most

familiar and most dear is three-fold. In the first place just *because* it is so familiar it has become inextricably part of one's own experience, of one's own very nature. And the self, the real "I", is incapable of description even if it were desirable. For the Christian it may not be difficult to describe the *contrast* between the old life and the new—if he has had that particular sharp moment of division between the two. I suppose the greatest of all such descriptions, and perhaps the most penetrating self-revelation in Christian literature, is that of an African: St Augustine of Hippo. But to convey what is loved whole-heartedly in a language which will convey that love and that meaning is beyond me. Equally, it is difficult to talk about home because it is precisely there, in that context, within the family, that the greatest influences and the greatest experiences of life are apt to be known and felt. Yet these are indescribable. How can a mother describe her love for her child? How can the bitterness of bereavement ever be fully expressed? There is, in all of us, a reticence and a reserve in talking of the greatest experiences of life: at least, I think, there ought to be.

But, finally, it has to be admitted, so much of what is familiar is taken for granted; so much of what home truly is in terms of security and comfort, of assurance and peace, is simply not noticed that it is impossible to speak of it with conviction. I sometimes think it a pity that the most familiar parable in the whole Gospel is called "the parable of the prodigal son". For, after all, there were *two* sons in that story, and we can often recognize ourselves behaving more like the elder than the younger. Or at least, I should say that I can. There he is, coming back along the path in the evening light. A path so familiar that he knows every twist and turn in it; almost every stone. So that, even when it grows dark he can recognize the outline of the trees, the dip in the ground that tells him he is almost there. But tonight there is something different. There is the noise of human voices, of music and dancing, of that hum of activity which comes from an excited crowd. And there are lights in the window. It is all so strange and so unfamiliar that, instead of going in by the usual way, he goes round to the back and calls a servant, asking him what has happened. "Haven't you heard? Your brother's come home—the one who was lost—and your father has ordered a feast; a calf has been killed and all the neighbours invited to rejoice." "And he was angry and would not go in." So his father comes to find him and to plead with him. But he turns on his father in fierce and bitter temper. "All these years I've sweated and slaved for you; kept the farm going; worked from morning to night in the fields; shown you that I know my duty as your son. And you never once offered me a feast. But as soon as that waster of a brother turns up you do everything to show your love for him; and you make certain, too, that everyone knows where your affections lie." And then those quiet words, "Son, you are always with me; *all that I have is yours.*" It is like that with

102

me, and perhaps with you too, with regard to all the blessings I have received from home.

But it is even more true, more literally true, of my life (and yours?) in the family of God; in the Church. "Son, you are always with me; all that I have is yours." That is the plain, simple fact of membership in the Body of Christ. And it is because of my constant acceptance and forgetfulness of it; it is because, through so many years, alas, I have taken it all for granted, that I find it hard to speak about it all to you. So let me begin at an easier point of departure; one which is familiar to us all.

What is the future of the Christian Church in Africa? An utterly impossible question, of course, as all questions about the future are bound to be. A question so full of ambiguities and possibilities and loose ends that it is hardly worth asking. And yet it *is* being asked. And it is being asked from within the Church as well as by those who, for differing reasons, look on outside. I cannot, of course, even begin to answer the question. But, if I am honest, I have to confess that it came to me again and again while I was bishop of an Anglican diocese in Africa.

I hear stories of the past; of all the splendidly faithful and heroic Christians who laboured to build up the family of God here and there in the diocese; and I look round and wonder if such people exist today. Or, on a different track altogether, I think of the peculiar and tremendously strong forces lying in wait, so to speak, for our simple Christians. Africa is a continent lying open to the ideological and secularist forces which are spreading over the whole earth. Won't the Christian religion—as it is now expressed in our villages—find it almost impossible to meet this challenge? Isn't there, perhaps, already a clear sign of failure in the attitude towards religion of the more highly educated young men and women in the diocese now; the secondary school boys, the teachers, the nurses and medical assistants? In any case, isn't it at least possible that the Christian faith has not got roots deep enough yet to withstand the storm and tempest? Are we too complacent; too ready to live our own sheltered Christian lives within the Christian family, but most unwilling to move out into the world around us and find new fields to conquer? Or is it—as it appears so clearly to be on the political level—that a Church which owed its first impetus to the European missionary effort cannot be the Church in Africa if there is still European initiative and leadership entrenched in it?

And what all these questions and imaginings amount to—even when they are justifiably part of a bishop's self-examination—is: are we Christians strong enough to look the future in the face? And so often the answer seems to come back—you know that you are not! And then, for me at least, there is the urgent need to think again about the very meaning of the Church, and I have to turn somewhere to find it: somewhere not too hopelessly dissimilar from my own situation. And there is a sentence or two in a letter written by St Paul to *his* little Christian family at Corinth, in those dawn-days so long ago, which always brings me strength again. Because it was written when the Christian Church was so tiny and insignificant that, humanly speaking, it hadn't a chance. Only a handful of men and women, scattered in little groups about the eastern Mediterranean. Most of them poor and ignorant people; many of them slaves. With all the vast pressures of a pagan empire at its prime weighing upon them. With a world of the intellect, formed by Greece, superbly disdainful of the nonsense, the foolishness they believed. With a Church, the Jewish Church, organized to destroy and defeat them whenever they laid claim to any religious truth. Christians—his little family—have until yesterday been regarded as the dregs of society in the most licentious city of the civilized world. Not exactly a situation of encouragement and hope for the man who sits down to write the letter. But this is what he says: "Even unto this present hour we both hunger and thirst and are naked and are buffeted, and have no certain dwelling place; and labour, working with our own hands. Being reviled, we bless; being persecuted, we suffer it; being defamed, we entreat; we are made as the filth of the world and are the offscouring of all things unto this day." And yet, "Thanks be to God, which giveth us the victory through our Lord Jesus Christ. . . . Be steadfast, unmovable, always abounding in the work of the Lord, for as much as you know that your labour is not in vain *in the Lord.*"

"In the Lord", "in Christ", words which recur again and again in St Paul's letters. And when he says "in Christ", St Paul refers, whether he knows it or not, to the Church. As Dr Knox has said, "The Christian life is a *koinonia* (a common life). Being a Christian is being a sharer, a participant. The reality in which the Christian shares is a reality in which others also share and is the reality it is because this is true."[1]

Sometimes it appears to the Christian that his experience, his knowledge of the truth that is in Jesus, is and must necessarily be a purely personal, purely individual thing. The touch of God cannot, he feels, be *mediated*; it is too intimate and too direct to be conceived of in this way. If it is, there must be some lessening of his own individual freedom; some barrier to his own individual response. Yet nothing could be less true. "Ultimately it is I myself who stand before God!" I quote Dr Knox again. "But the God before whom I consciously stand as a Christian, although I cannot sense his presence without knowing that it fills all of heaven and earth, was nevertheless in his particular character revealed only in a *communal* Event and continues to be revealed only in the communal existence in which the Event is remembered and in a sense constantly recurrent . . ."[2] "The Word

[1] Knox, *The Church and the Reality of Christ*, p. 118.
[2] Knox, p. 128.

God spoke in history was nothing other than the calling of this new community into being . . . we remember Jesus because we share in the Church's memory . . . what we know as the reconciling act of God in him [that act made clear to man on the hill of Golgotha] was the creation around him of the community of love and hope to which we belong . . . we can speak of Christ's continuing presence only because we know the mystery and the glory of the Church's own true life."[3]

Is not this too large a claim to make for the organized, institutional historic Church that we know today? Is not this claim for the Church to deny, in fact, the infinitude, the eternity of God's reconciling work? Is not this to *limit* God to something which is, even if his work, a human and most fallible instrument as well? No doubt it would be if we thought of God's work in the Church simply confined to history; to this moment of time or that. But so it would be also, if we limited the work of God to history itself. God's plan is not so restricted. To the scope or range of God's action in Christ St Paul sees no limit whatever. "The good news of the unfathomable riches of Christ", "the hidden purpose", for all mankind "was hidden for long ages in God the Creator of the universe, in order that now, *through the Church*, the wisdom of God might be made known to the rulers and authorities in the realms of *heaven*." True, that the Church, in its earthly condition, is bound to

---

[3] Knox, p. 129.

be limited. True, that the Church, at any one moment in history or in any one place—in Africa as much as in America, in Russia as much as in Australia—is restricted by the very fact that it is composed of flesh and blood. But it is our knowing "in part" which alone gives rise to the expectation that "we shall know even as we are known". "Whatever God may have in store for us—and we shall be confident that it is beyond our capacity to know or even to imagine—what he now *offers* us in Christ is offered only through a human Event and a human community."[4]

Yet there is another objection, and a potent one. Where is the Church? How do we identify it? Isn't the present disunity and discordance an impossible obstacle to my acceptance of the Church as the means of glory?

Wasn't Archbishop William Temple right when he said, as he is reputed to have done, "I believe in the Holy Catholic and Apostolic Church, but sincerely regret that it does not exist"? Clearly (and we have Christ's own word for it) the disunity of the Christian Church is the greatest single obstacle to faith. "The world" will not—perhaps more truly *cannot*— "believe" until a visible, external unity in accordance with the mind of Christ is restored. But even assessing the present "unhappy divisions" at their worst; even granting their existence to be a proof of Christian sinfulness and hardness of heart; even

[4] Knox, p. 119.

accepting the fact that they distort utterly the true nature of the Body of Christ; still, these divisions are *within*—in the true sense—the one Body, and not outside it. William Temple was wrong, not because he recognized and deplored the horror of disunity; but because, in this remembered sentence at least, he looked upon the Church as if it were an ideal reality, not an actual present historical fact. The fact falls short of the ideal, therefore it does not exist. But the Church, one, holy, Catholic, apostolic, *does* exist; as much today as nineteen hundred years ago. And what Christians have to do—and, thank God, *are* doing with increasing conviction and determination—is to try to set the existing Church free to be itself more fully. This is the meaning of all ecumenical effort, because it is the meaning also of all Christian hope.

But in the meanwhile what is my own personal attitude to be? Or rather, what am I to do, if I wish to respond to Christ's call? Is it still possible to find a clue to the nature of the Christian life which can be mine—now? The earliest account of the Christian life is this:

"They met constantly to hear the apostles teach, and to share the common life, to break bread, and to pray."[5] To listen: to share: to break bread.

Even in our dividedness, we can do these things. If we do not do them, our dividedness will remain

[5] Acts 2:42.

and grow deeper. "To hear the apostles teach": that is to say, to recognize joyfully and thankfully that we are all learners, and shall be to the end of our earthly life. And that, because we are so, we must be humble enough to accept authority within the Church and to see in it a part of the Lord's plan and purpose.

"To share the common life": because that *is* the Christian life, and without it, Christian faith and practice are impossible.

"To break bread": liturgy. The act by which, from the very first, the Christian community recognized the continuing presence of the Lord; shared in "his full perfect and sufficient sacrifice, oblation and satisfaction" for the sins of the whole world; knew the power of his resurrection.

"*To pray*": adoration; the acknowledgement of the fact of God, almighty, all-holy, all-loving—and of myself as his creature. Penitence: the truth about myself—"be merciful to me, a sinner". Thanksgiving: the truth about my human, earthly existence; about my relationship to God himself. "All that I have is thine." Petition and intercession: the showing of my poverty and need; the showing also of the poverty and need of my neighbour and of my love for him.

This is the life of the Church. This is the life of the Christian. And there is no other. This is power and this is glory.

Now to him who is able to do immeasurably more than all we can ask or conceive, by the power which is at work among us, to him be glory in the Church and in Christ Jesus from generation to generation evermore!

9

The True and Living God

*These last two addresses were given
during a mission to Oxford University
in 1963*

In choosing as the title of these addresses "The
True and Living God" I have a double purpose. On
the one hand I want to emphasize my belief in
the emptiness, the unreality, the "absurdity" (to
use a phrase of Jean-Paul Sartre) of life as lived
by modern Western man. On the other, I want to
proclaim as the foundation of the whole Christian apologia that it answers this absurdity with
Truth and this emptiness with Life. And I want
to attempt to show you this, not by an appeal
to philosophy in the abstract or to theology in
the abstract, but by an appeal to experience. I
recognize the dangers! This kind of approach must
mean that I speak about myself; and therefore it
can look horribly like plain arrogance. Moreover,
it must mean that I speak about my own experience—particular, partial, limited, and therefore
perhaps irrelevant to a large area of life, the area in
which *you* live. Finally, it must mean that I cannot *prove* my case to you: that I cannot prove it at

the deepest level when we shall be thinking about the existence of God or his nature; that I cannot prove it at the level of everyday situations and confrontations, when we shall be thinking about such things as sex and ambition and vocation and hydrogen bombs and loneliness. I can only answer that, because the cause is so tremendous and the choice before you so desperately urgent, I must take risks. And I am much comforted by the fact that that is precisely what Jesus Christ told his closest friends to do. "If you want to follow me," he said, "you had better forget all about security": whether the security of home life ("unless you hate your father and mother and brothers and sisters, don't come after me") or the security of a job ("look at the flowers . . . the birds . . . nature: and stop worrying about where your next meal is coming from") or, even, security from the tempest of passion and desire ("follow me . . . look at me . . . I offer you nothing in the way of comfort or ease or freedom from buffeting . . . I offer you a gallows, a total loss, failure . . .") The element of risk in the Christian religion is not something which passes away as one grows older, for it lies at the heart of the faith itself. A religion whose symbol is the cross is the religion which warns men off if they are timid about life—at least it ought to! Perhaps one of the reasons why it is necessary to have a mission in the University of Oxford is simply because that symbol, so evident everywhere on our buildings, has ceased to have reality and meaning as itself. Christianity has become, as we are so often nowadays reminded, part of the Establishment. And there is no room for a cross there!

But, to return to the main theme of these addresses, The True and Living God—the God, that is, who secures to man a changeless, unchanging, immutable standard by which all else can be judged and valued. The God, that is, who is operative *in* the world, not merely in the lives of men and women who believe in him, not merely in the institution called the Church, but in the whole of life. So that there is no single part of human experience which lies outside the range of his influence and power: so that all mankind's most glorious adventures, from reaching for the stars to probing for the origins of being, are his concern. The True and Living God! Standing over against the shadows which are taken for reality in our generation—power, affluence, prestige, at the personal and the international level. Standing over against the deadness which spreads through society when, as today, it yields to a view of itself based on materialism and determinism, a society of ants or formulae. The True and Living God! The God, that is, to whom the vastness of the universe and the minuteness of the atom are standards of size without meaning: for to his infinity they are without comparison. Their truth, unlike his truth, being relative to the human mind which explores and measures them. And so the God whom man can know and adore, because in him is life.

I have expanded my title at length not because

I want to pre-judge your own choice or your own consideration of the claims of Christianity, but simply to begin by making as clear as I can the reasons which led me to choose it. For it seems to me that if my mission is to be of any use, it can only be so by presenting the issues straight and arguing them out. I come to you as a Christian. It would be ridiculous, and dishonest too, if I were to pretend to approach the contemporary world as one unaffected by that background and that conviction. It is my life. I have no other. But I hope you will believe that, just because I have been and am involved in this contemporary world with you, I share your problems and feel myself most intimately concerned with them.

Perhaps my only real justification for daring to undertake these addresses is that I have been rather closely involved with what is, after all, one of the major issues of our world: the rise of African nationalism and the tremendous challenge of race relations. No one living and working in any part of Africa today can be outside the contemporary situation. He is involved, whether he likes it or not, whether he understands it or not, in one of the greatest revolutions of history. Moreover, he is bound, if he has any intelligence at all, to see that revolution against the broader perspective of world movements. Perhaps the danger is, for us who have the good luck to be in Africa today, to think too much in terms of our own vast continent. But at least it means we cannot go to sleep and forget the world itself.

I recall an evening during my ministry in Tanzania in a little village called Huwe, not far from the great Ruvuma River. I had come there for the first time earlier in the day, and been greeted by the whole village with true African hospitality and friendship. There were speeches and gifts of eggs and chickens, and there was a fascinating dance by masked dancers. In the evening, after supper, I sat outside my hut and the people gathered round in the moonlight to talk. Because I knew it would amuse them, I brought out my portable transistor set and tuned in to the news. What I heard was the voice of Major Gagarin, speaking from outer space: the voice of the first man to make that incredible adventure. And I could not begin to explain what it meant to the people sitting at my feet. Yet Gagarin and they and I were of the same world, of the same flesh.

The first, and most obvious, fact of our world is this great leap forward in scientific achievement and technological advance. A leap so vast, and so rapid, that mankind as a whole cannot adjust itself to it quickly enough. But it is a leap that has been taken. Man has no choice but to adjust. Inevitably such an achievement as the mastery of space travel gives to mankind a new sense of power and of freedom. It opens a new dimension. There is apparently no limit, after all, to exploration and discovery. Yet, at the same time, we know that the very qualities and skills which make such advances possible also make possible the Bomb and the Balance of Terror in whose shadow we all live. It is a world of hope and of despair. Perhaps it has always been so. But today, because it is so inescapably one world, because we are so dependent upon one another, because we can know, within seconds, what is happening anywhere on earth and how it will affect us, we are more immediately conscious of this tension and of this paradox.

Yet I do not think, for Western civilization at least, that this is the most significant factor of our age. Surely that lies closer to the heart of man himself: to the way in which he thinks of life itself: of the environment which gives him the only answers there appear to be. More important than Einstein, for our generation, are Marx and Freud. It is they who have created the intellectual climate in which modern man lives and moves and has his being. And this is true for those who accept and believe—as I do myself—that each was making a vitally important break-through in the analysis of society and of the working of human nature, as for those who see only falsehood and evil in their discoveries. The consequence of what they discovered is, however, a world without freedom, a life without choice, an "absurdity" in which man is always the victim of his environment or of heredity.

I try to keep abreast of what is going on in Europe by reading reviews of plays and novels: where possible by reading the novels themselves. And, inescapably, I get this impression of a civilization haunted by the sense that life is meaningless, a farce, a dirty joke. Perhaps this assessment is true for intellectuals only. But I think that the ordinary man, the ordinary undergraduate, is conscious of being the victim of forces only half understood: of movements of society over which there is no control: of his own unconscious to which, apparently, there is no access but which determines the course of his life and of his relationship with others. Whether by society or by the unconscious, life is determined: man is enslaved: there is no point in struggling to shape your own destiny: that has been decided. All you can do is to wait for Godot. And so, finally, ours is a world in which there appear to be no fixed standards of right and wrong any longer. Everything is relative, for everything has to be judged against this background of forces, social and personal, beyond man's control. So, internationally, truth becomes always secondary to expediency. It is less moral to observe an agreement than to move forward into greater power. So, individually, it is less moral to observe a promise ". . . till death us do part" than to find fulfilment with another, and part without recrimination.

In all I have been saying it may seem as if I take a very gloomy, very pessimistic view of the modern world. And perhaps it is that, living in Africa, and confronted day by day with simpler, more fundamental problems of human existence—what has to do with food and water and the development of natural resources—one feels a sense of loss for our Western civilizations.

Certainly one gets pretty desperate at the thought that, inescapably, Africa is part of this world: is increasingly influenced by it: has her destiny linked to it whatever she may wish or will to do. But I think there is enough truth in what I have said for it to be recognizable. A world of hope and of despair: a world of forces against which the person struggles in vain: a world of shadows and unreality.

And over against this The True and Living God. Here is the choice. We call him the Creator. We mean by this, not that he made the Universe at some point far away in time and left it to develop according to its own fixed laws. We mean, rather, that the whole Universe and everything within it, animate and inanimate, is dependent, has the quality (I cannot speak in philosophical language) of "creatureliness": of developing or evolving in accordance with the will of its creator from moment to moment. We mean by this that individuality, the individuality of the sparrow as much as of the human being, is the direct concern of the Creator. We mean that every human discovery, in the cosmic dimension or elsewhere, is a discovery of some part of that creative process: is, in the truest sense, a gift from the Creator as well as a striving from the side of the Creature. And therefore we believe that man is made for adoration: and that without this he is inevitably and inescapably less than man. It is the acknowledgement of dependence, of creatureliness, that alone can make sense of the world: for this is the very first law of its being.

Without God, Marx and Freud are right. We have no freedom, we are slaves ... "for that we exchange the truth of God for a lie and worship and serve the Creature rather than the Creator ... " and one must pay the price.

Of course, I cannot prove it to you. I can only try to describe it. I can only say "Try and see". And here again I am bound to be personal and to run the appalling risk of arrogance. I can only talk to you out of my own experience: it is all I have. There is such a danger of thinking that these words of mine about God, about the Creator, about his Creation, are all very well but have no relevance to contemporary issues—so why should they be relevant to me, here, today?

But you see, one inescapable consequence of thinking about God as Creator is the realization that he *cares*, and that his caring reaches across all the barriers of colour and race and tribe erected by man. And another consequence of this doctrine is that the caring is for each individual, attractive or unattractive: clever or stupid: rich or poor. And the most important consequence of all is that this Creature, by definition, belongs to and is made for his Creator. So that anything, or anyone, which interferes with his dignity as a person is in effect denying the sovereignty and purposes of God: is a blasphemer. When you are fighting against racial prejudice, or when you are striving to help forward a young country and its people, you need more than a theory, more than some good ideas.

At least, I know I do. It is the knowledge, the certainty, that this is God's world, that these are his creatures, his children, his final purposes, that alone sustains me. Without it, I could see no point in anything that I have done or could do.

"We worship and adore the framer and former of the Universe; governor, disposer, keeper; him on whom all things depend; mind and spirit of the world; from whom all things spring; by whose spirit we live; the divine spirit diffused through all; God all-powerful; God always present; God above all other gods: thee we worship and adore."

10

The Hard Core

At the end of Rose Macaulay's book, *The Towers of Trebizond*, Aunt Dot says to her niece, whose lover has been killed in a car smash . . . "I know you read Clement of Alexandria: do you remember where he says, "We may not be taken up and transported to our journey's end, but must travel thither on foot, traversing the whole distance of the narrow way?" One mustn't lose sight of the *hard core* which is, do this, do that . . . understand the world you live in and be on terms with it, don't dramatize and dream of *escape*."

The hard core of Christianity is what we have been trying to think about: that, set in the context of the world we live in. I recognize only too clearly that my own attempts to describe this hard core and to make it relevant have been very unworthy and feeble. And, moreover, I am horribly aware of the difficulty in our world of "communication" between Christians and non-Christians, even between one generation and another. "Understand the world you live in" was easier for those of Aunt Dot's generation than it is for us. For, whatever else may be said, it *is* a more complicated world just because we know so much more about it: just because our knowledge of it is so immediate and without time for reflection. And, because it is complicated, it is perhaps easier to take a gloomy view of it than it used to be. Not only because we have lost our belief in an automatic progress to better and better goals and fulfilments, but because of the real and constant problems which haunt us and cast deep shadows.

Many of these are so obvious, so present to us, that I hardly need to mention them again. The *fear* consequent upon a divided world—divided by differing ideologies, divided between rich and poor, divided by emergent nationalisms. The fear of the *power* that man has himself discovered and can unleash at will. The fear of *vastness* all about us, and our own littleness. The loneliness that all these fears can bring into the human heart.

But fundamentally, because theologically—because, if we may dare to express it so, from God's point of view—the world "is very good". And man, because he is man, God's creature, made in God's image and likeness, is also "very good". And the things he uses and the things he knows and discovers and invents, because they also are God's creatures, are "very good".

This is not fantasy or escapism, nor is it a denial of the realities of Evil and of Sin and of Death. It is simply the assertion of truth about Creation and man as part of Creation. It says nothing of the use that he can make of it if, in his freedom, he so chooses. It sets the mystery of Evil—however we may care to meet that mystery—in the context of a world that is still, and will be till the end of time, God's world. And it can make a difference to the way in which we approach that world and live in it.

In the first place, if we believe that it *is* God's world, we must rejoice in it and expect it to be capable of *enriching* life. Here is the first great paradox of Christianity. We are pledged by our baptismal promises "to renounce the world, the flesh and the devil". But this world that we renounce is, precisely, society organized apart from God: is what we understand by the adjective "worldly" in the pejorative sense. The very renunciation of this world leaves us the more free to rejoice in and to love God's creation—the world which, in everything, bears the traces of his hands and is a continuous reminder of his uncreated loveliness. St Francis of Assisi—the saint most familiar even to our generation—expresses this truth and the paradox that lies behind it. Renunciation: he casts away the wealth and the prestige that are his own worldly heritage, together with the clothes of silk and satin that he throws at his father's feet. He loves his Lady Poverty and follows her to the ends of the earth. He "bears in his body the marks of the Lord Jesus". But he is the most world-affirming saint in history: rejoicing in every creature: personalizing every creature (even Death) because he finds in them the person of their Creator.

Perhaps the subtlest temptation of this age—at least here in Europe—is the temptation to despair.

If we really "understand the world we live in" and know it to be still God's world, then we are of all men the most hopeful. "Marvellous are thy works: and that my soul knoweth right well."

*

Therefore, too, we may not only rejoice in this world's goods, but expect to find a purpose and a meaning in it: a purpose and a meaning not *in spite of* the complexity of things—as though we had to push our way through life, like pushing our way through uncleared jungle—but because of the richness and variety of them. We are not created to be men always "waiting for Godot"—seeing nothing but the passage of time and the meaninglessness of existence. "For all that may be known of God by men lies plain before their eyes", wrote the Apostle Paul to the little group of Christian converts in the centre of the world, "indeed God himself has disclosed it to them. His invisible attributes, that is to say, his everlasting power and deity, have been visible ever since the world began . . . in the things he has made. . . .Knowing God, they have refused to honour him as God or to render him thanks. *Hence* all their thinking has ended in futility."

If all is held in God's hands, is part of Divine wisdom and purpose, then not only can life never be futile, never be meaningless, but it must be invested with a purpose and a meaning so tremendous that it often overwhelms us. Only after the event, only at the top of the ridge, can we pause and look back and understand.

*

But we must not ask of the world what it cannot give. We must not ask this even of a world which is "very good" and which is God's creation, sustained by his "everlasting power and deity". The men of an earlier generation had a far greater sense of the transience of things than we have. To them the thought of man as a stranger and a pilgrim here on earth, with "no abiding city", was as familiar as the thought of death as the gateway to life and joy and peace. It is because of this possessiveness in our attitude to life that we often create our own unhappiness and our own deepest pains and sorrows. We must not ask of the world permanence, changelessness, constancy—for these are not the attributes of the creature but of the Creator with whom alone "is no variableness, neither shadow of turning". And if we expect these things and plan and build our life as if they were present, part of the world's fabric and being, then we are certain to lose our way. Every year, on Ash Wednesday, in some village or other of my diocese I went to celebrate the Eucharist. And as the people knelt on the mud floor in front of me, in a church built of earth and wood and thatch, I used the ancient words of the Liturgy and made the sign of the Cross on their foreheads with the ashes: "Remember, O Man, that dust thou art, and unto dust shalt thou return. . . . " Morbid? Medieval? Misanthropic?

No—just the plain and simple truth. We were there, together, my people and I. But we were only strangers and pilgrims, with no continuing city. The building around us—it will one day return to the dust from which it was made. The floor on which we knelt—perhaps thousands of knees will make their imprint on the dust, but the day will come when it too will return and be unrecognized. And the bodies who knelt in front of me, old men and young women and the babies on their backs peering up at me as I pass . . . "Dust thou art, and unto dust shalt thou return." But he whom they knelt to worship, for whom they were created, he will remain the object of that worship for ever. "Whom have I in heaven but thee, and there is none upon earth"—none, and nothing that I desire in comparison of thee.

*

My function has been chiefly to provide "a hard core" for you to build on. But I realize that I have not done this so much in terms of actual, hard practicalities, as in ideas. Now I want you to consider the words of Christ as the "hard core" of your own personal, individual vocation. I have chosen these verses because they seem to me to contain *all* that we need to know for this purpose.

(a) *Jesus knowing that his hour was come that he should depart out of this world unto the Father, having loved his own which was in the world, he loved them unto the end (EIS TELOS).*

Jesus, knowing that the Father had given all things into his hands and that he came forth from God and goeth unto God . . .

Jesus, in other words, *knowing* with a perfection and a completeness that were absolute: *loving* with a love that is perfect and all-embracing—in the light of this knowledge and of this love "riseth from supper, and layeth aside his garments: and took a towel and girded himself . . . and began to wash the disciples' feet."

It is significant that this incident of the feet-washing—described with such care and such an eye for detail that it cannot but be the description of an eye-witness—takes the place, in St John, of the action by which the Lord instituted his Eucharist. It is, in fact, a way of interpreting that Eucharist and of laying bare its inner meaning, not only to the disciples but—if they are faithful—to the world.

Jesus "laid aside his garments"—his garments of glory and of godhead—and "girded himself" with swaddling clothes in the manger: with a purple robe and a crown of thorns before Herod: with the nakedness and stripping of Golgotha—and "washed their feet"—the feet that are hot and sweaty and dusty with the dirt of the world's streets upon them.

(b) *And Simon Peter said, "Thou shalt never wash my feet." "If I wash thee not thou hast no part with me".*

This is the first condition of Christian disciple-
ship —the recognition that we are in need of
cleansing: the recognition that always, and in
every way we go, we go as sinners, as penitents,
and not as the righteous who need no repentance.

What in fact is the quality most needed in a
world like ours? A world where man is so haunted
and so lonely and so afraid? It is not enough to
bring to the service of such a world the qualities
of generosity or of understanding alone—
desperately as these are needed. For man's condition today needs above all else *compassion*,
"suffering with"—"when he came where he was",
there, half-dead and bleeding in the ditch. But
you cannot have compassion without penitence.
"If I wash thee not, thou hast no part with me."
Now penitence is not an emotional reaction—nor
is it a desperately complicated spiritual exercise.
It is something which lies within the reach of
every one of us who is capable of loving. It is
love. It is an act of the will by which love turns
to God again, and, having turned, accepts. "Lord
not my feet only . . . "

(c) *So when he had washed their feet he said
unto them, "Know ye what I have done to
you? Ye call me Master and Lord: and ye say
well—for so I am."*

He is *the Lord*: the Lord of all life, the Master
of each one who in penitence acknowledges him.

And therefore the first duty of the Christian is *worship*, and the most important work of the Christian is *prayer*. Worship—the acknowledgement of that Lordship, that Sovereignty: and, because we are members one of another, the expression of it corporately as a *worshipping community*.

Even in a divided and fragmented Christendom, even in spite of the scandal of disunity which is still our greatest scandal and greatest stumbling-block in confronting the world, we have preserved corporateness in our own different traditions. Our first duty, surely, is to make *this* corporateness more real, more informed with charity, more of a witness to the love of God which we have known and experienced. And the way to this is faithfulness in common worship. There is no such thing as private prayer. "Ye call me Master and Lord." ... Prayer is the supreme way of Christian Action—not a sort of escapist substitute for doing nothing. The Christian faith itself implies "that the kingdom of God is to be promoted in human history by no other power than the power of love" and "the power of God's love takes effect in human history in no other way than through the wills and actions of men in whom that love has come to dwell. To pray is to open the heart to the entry of love."

Of course, it is not easy to pray. Most people who give up prayer do so not because it is perplexing or dark in meaning, but because it is so hard. It is work. It is action. It is demanding: "It is not easy", writes John Burnaby "to believe that prayer is either always or never answered in the way desired. It is possible–indeed necessary—to believe that true Christian prayer is always the service of God."[1] "Ye call me Master and Lord: and ye say well, for so *I am*."

(d) *"If I then, the Lord and the Master, have washed your feet, ye also ought to wash one another's feet. . . . A servant is not greater than his lord; neither one that is sent greater than he that sent him . . . "*

Service. It is a word too easily used by Christians if they forget what it really means. "He took a towel"—it was the outward badge of slavery, of humiliation. "He girded himself"—made the humiliation a reality, by laying aside the garments of his glory and clothing himself with the garments of mortal flesh. "He washed their feet"—the action, the activity, of the slave: disregarded by those for whom it was done, unrewarded by thanks or recognition of any kind: at worst, disgusting; at best, a drudgery.

So the action of Christians which must flow from their penitence and their worship is *service.* And it is "enough for the disciple that he be as his master, and the servant as his lord".

I have come to you from Africa. From one of the countries in Africa just at the beginning of its history as a sovereign independent state. But I

[1] J. BURNABY, *Soundings*, pp.232–3

have also had experience of other parts of the great continent, richer and more powerful, yet infinitely less hopeful and less happy. Africa needs, with a very great urgency, the *service* of the Christian Church. Today, more even than a hundred years ago, is the day of opportunity. For now we have the chance of contributing to the full and free development of new nations: nations of immense vitality and hopefulness: nations which recognize the divided world in which they are compelled to live, but which, in the case of the vast majority, desire above all to contribute to the healing of division. But countries like Tanzania, potentially so rich in human skills and abilities, have been left desperately poor, at the beginning of their day of freedom, in trained manpower. This is, perhaps, the most devastating criticism of colonialism—that it did not care sufficiently, or did not act in time, to give back to Africa, in exchange for so much material benefit and power, the skills it could so easily have taught. I speak of Africa, for it is the place I know and the place I love. But I speak for all countries in need of development: for all lands confronted—as Tanzania is—with the three enemies: poverty, ignorance and disease. What a field for Christian service! But only if it really *is* service, and not a disguised form of the the thing which seeks privilege or power or even, only thanks.

It must be as servants of Africa that we come: recognizing that we have no claim at all to any other position. The towel must be our badge, and it must be girded close around us. And the skills we bring—as doctors or as teachers or as technicians—these are the instruments of our service: the basin and the water, if you like, which we must use for the task. It is to no purpose coming to Africa to serve if you have not the tools of your service—and it may mean years of preparation, perhaps, before you acquire them.

But neither the service, nor the skills — the towel nor the water—will avail anything without faith: to transpose a context a little—"the substance of things *hoped for*, the evidence of things *not seen*". To be able to go and to give and to use: and at the end of it all, whether after a few years or a lifetime, to be dispensable: this is the faith you require. "The servant is not greater than his lord, nor he that is sent than he that sent him." To the worker, the end of that life of service, the moment of completion and consummation appeared to be, and indeed truly was, a single cry in the darkness, from a gallows.

*

But I hope I am not so foolish as to limit Christian service to one form of activity or to one part of God's world. I am aware, for one thing, of the pace of change: of the fact that in ten years' time, or even in five, our world may be a totally different world, and the claims upon Christian compassion and Christian faith will be different too. I am also aware that, even now, I am addressing persons with widely differing aptitudes, characters and talents. It would be an intolerable insult to assume a sort of mass-opinion which could be swayed in one direction or another by some appeal to its generosity. I am aware, above all, that what is right for one may be wrong for another: and that vocation—the Christian vocation at least—must be understood against a background of diversity: of persons, each with his own particular and special place to fill in God's world and in God's purposes.

Service overseas—but also here—in the persons of those who are at once the product of our social order and the "outsiders"—the maladjusted children, the alcoholics, the neurotics, the delinquents and criminals, the lonely and aged . . .

Vocation! Is there really any way of saying to an audience what it means to each one within that audience:

Vocation! It is—somehow—like "service" or "commitment", a rather dangerous word. It is so easy to talk, and even to think, of "*my* vocation"—as though it was something upon which I confer a dignity and a glory by accepting it.

But what is it really? Once again—remember Early Church: Dawn. Laodicea is one of them— the least attractive, not unlike some of our Christian churches today. "I know thy works, that thou art neither cold nor hot . . . so because thou art lukewarm, and neither hot nor cold, I will spue thee out of my mouth." Not a very encouraging thing to hear. And it gets even worse. "Thou sayest, I am rich (and have gotten riches) and have need of nothing; and knowest not that thou art wretched and miserable and poor and blind and naked."

Yet it is to *this* church: to this group of Christians—lukewarm in their faith, wretched, miserable, poor, blind and naked in their life as Christians—that the most winning words in the whole of Scripture are addressed:

"Behold, I stand at the door and knock: if any man hear my voice and open the door, I will come in to him and will sup with him, and he with me."

Vocation! What is it—really? *My* life? *My* activity? *My* decision? *My* way?

It is none of these. It is Jesus, the Lord, the True and Living God, standing, knocking, waiting. That is all.

Hope and Suffering
Desmond Tutu

"Here . . . is the authentic voice of Christian prophecy in our day. Unafraid to proclaim . . . the truth about apartheid . . . to challenge . . . the assault on human rights . . . to risk the consequences for himself . . . But always in hope: always in love: always in the certainty that God is present . . ."

Trevor Huddleston

Naught for Your Comfort
Trevor Huddleston

The book that foretold the Soweto uprising and stirred the conscience of the world . . .

Instrument of Thy Peace
Alan Paton

"Worthy of a permanent place on the short shelf of enduring classics of the life of the Spirit."

Henry P. Van Dusan,
Union Theological Seminary

Let My People Go
Albert Luthuli

"Luthuli's love for his country transcends his loyalty to any one racial group within it. This book will surely convince the world that the Nobel Prize was most justly awarded to its author."

Trevor Huddleston

Also available in Fount Paperbacks

I Believe
Trevor Huddleston

A simple, prayerful series of reflections on the phrases of the Creed. This is a beautiful testament of the strong, quiet inner faith of a man best known for his active role in the Church – and in the world.

The Heart of the Christian Faith
Donald Coggan

The author ". . . presents the essential core of Christianity in a marvellously simple and readable form, quite uncluttered by any excess of theological technicality."
The Yorkshire Post

Be Still and Know
Michael Ramsey

The former Archbishop of Canterbury looks at prayer in the New Testament, at what the early mystics could teach us about it, and at some practical aspects of Christian praying.

Pilgrim's Progress
John Bunyan

"A masterpiece which generation after generation of ordinary men and women have taken to their hearts."
Hugh Ross Williamson

Also available in Fount Paperbacks

BOOKS BY C. S. LEWIS

The Abolition of Man

'It is the most perfectly reasoned defence of Natural Law (Morality) I have ever seen, or believe to exist.'

Walter Hooper

Mere Christianity

'He has a quite unique power for making theology an attractive, exciting and fascinating quest.'

Times Literary Supplement

God in the Dock

'This little book . . . consists of some brilliant pieces . . . This is just the kind of book to place into the hands of an intellectual doubter . . . It has been an unalloyed pleasure to read.'

Marcus Beverley, Christian Herald

The Great Divorce

'Mr Lewis has a rare talent for expressing spiritual truth in fresh and striking imagery and with uncanny acumen . . . it contains many flashes of deep insight and exposures of popular fallacies.'

Church Times

Also available in Fount Paperbacks

The Mind of St Paul
WILLIAM BARCLAY

'There is a deceptive simplicity about this fine exposition of
Pauline thought at once popular and deeply theological. The
Hebrew and Greek backgrounds are described and all the main
themes are lightly but fully treated.'   *The Yorkshire Post*

The Plain Man Looks at the Beatitudes
WILLIAM BARCLAY

'. . . the author's easy style should render it . . . valuable and
acceptable to the ordinary reader.'   *Church Times*

The Plain Man Looks at the Lord's Prayer
WILLIAM BARCLAY

Professor Barclay shows how this prayer that Jesus gave to his
disciples is at once a summary of Christian teaching and a
pattern for all prayers.

The Plain Man's Guide to Ethics
WILLIAM BARCLAY

The author demonstrates beyond all possible doubt that the
Ten Commandments are the most relevant document in the
world today and are totally related to mankind's capacity to
live and make sense of it all within a Christian context.

Ethics in a Permissive Society
WILLIAM BARCLAY

How do we as Christians deal with such problems as drug
taking, the 'pill', alcohol, morality of all kinds, in a society
whose members are often ignorant of the Church's teaching?
Professor Barclay approaches a difficult and vexed question
with his usual humanity and clarity, asking what Christ himself
would say or do in our world today.

Fount Paperbacks

Fount is one of the leading paperback publishers of religious books and below are some of its recent titles.

- [ ] GETHSEMANE Martin Israel   £2.50
- [ ] HIS HEALING TOUCH Michael Buckley   £2.50
- [ ] YES TO LIFE David Clarke   £2.95
- [ ] THE DIVORCED CATHOLIC Edmund Flood   £1.95
- [ ] THE WORLD WALKS BY Sue Masham   £2.95
- [ ] C. S. LEWIS: THE MAN AND HIS GOD
      Richard Harries   £1.75
- [ ] BEING FRIENDS Peter Levin   £2.95
- [ ] DON'T BE AFRAID TO SAY YOU'RE LONELY
      Christopher Martin   £2.50
- [ ] BASIL HUME: A PORTRAIT Tony Castle (ed.)   £3.50
- [ ] TERRY WAITE: MAN WITH A MISSION
      Trevor Barnes   £2.95
- [ ] PRAYING THROUGH PARADOX Charles Elliott   £2.50
- [ ] TIMELESS AT HEART C. S. Lewis   £2.50
- [ ] THE POLITICS OF PARADISE Frank Field   £3.50
- [ ] THE WOUNDED CITY Trevor Barnes   £2.50
- [ ] THE SACRAMENT OF THE WORD Donald Coggan   £2.95
- [ ] IS THERE ANYONE THERE? Richard MacKenna   £1.95

All Fount paperbacks are available through your bookshop or newsagent, or they can be ordered by post from Fount Paperbacks, Cash Sales Department, G.P.O. Box 29, Douglas, Isle of Man. Please send purchase price plus 22p per book, maximum postage £3. Customers outside the UK send purchase price, plus 22p per book. Cheque, postal order or money order. No currency.

NAME (Block letters)_____

ADDRESS _____

_____

_____